D1151083

Cooking with Daisy

Josie Klafkowska with photographs by Pip Calvert

Quercus

Acknowledgements

There are so many people that I need to thank for their part in the creation of *Cooking with Daisy*. I should probably start with all of the mothers, fathers and grandmothers that have provided such a wonderful collection of recipes. Without all of you, I would never even have got to first base. Thank you.

This book also includes recipes donated by chefs, celebrities and food writers. My sincere thanks go, in no particular order, to Emma Forbes, Roopa Gulati, Mary Cadogan, Ruth Watson, Silvana Franco, Gary Lineker, Antony Worrall Thompson, Clare Gordon-Smith, Sue Lawrence, Brian Turner, Nigel Slater, Nigella Lawson, Fiona Beckett, Delia Smith, Wendy Turner, Lindsay Nicholson, Shona Crawford Poole and Orla Broderick. A very big and special thank you goes to Lorna Wing for putting me in touch with so many of these people and for advice and encouragement when I needed it.

Thanks must go also to my team of testers and their children who assisted in trying out each and every recipe that appears in the book.

Next, I must thank my wonderful models and their parents: George and Edward Cozens; Enzo Allen; Holly and Kitty Edwards; Oliver and Louisa Smith; Matty Beatty; Madeleine and Ben Haynes; Alexander Blaxall; Giorgio Caldesi; Richard and Patrick Nolan; Harvey and Tom Lewis; Oliver, Alessandra and Thomas Nelson-Smith; Francesca Daley; Rosie Gandon; Venice and Emil Farr; Yannick Emilien; Sophie Sargent; Evie Faber; Sam Willis; Augusta Williams; and Tom and Alice Whitting.

Thanks to the parents of all of these children but particularly to those that let us invade their kitchens: Julia and Steve Haynes; Victoria and Chris Smith; Katie and Giancarlo Caldesi; Jane and Charles Cozens; Nicky Sargent; and Liz and Carsten Edwards; with particular thanks to Liz Edwards for her baking, styling and organisational skills.

I would definitely have given up at the halfway post were it not for the support of Jason and Charlotte Maude and Joseph Britto, founders of The Isabel Medical Charity. Thank you so much for offering financial support and for pushing me forwards when I needed it.

This book would be nothing without its stunning photography. I am indebted to Pip Calvert, my very good friend and photographer for her talent, time, determination and patience and to Flash Photography for developing so many wonderful photographs. Thanks also to Annie Rigg for adding her experience and helping us to make some of the dishes look so good.

I am equally indebted to Anthony Michael and Stephanie Nash and to their team at Michael Nash Design for their creative genius. They committed to bringing *Cooking with Daisy* to life without thinking twice. Thank you.

Ben Barton had never met me when he decided to commit himself to getting *Cooking with Daisy* published. He gave his time and energy without hesitation and, for that, I am extremely grateful. Enormous thanks go to Anthony Cheetham who never gave up on me and to Smith Davies Publishing for retaining their faith in the idea. Thank you also to Graham Arthur and his colleagues at Covington & Burling for legal advice.

Thanks aren't really enough for Rosan Meyer. Her knowledge and expertise has made this book what it is and her unstinting support since the day we met has been incredible. What can I say?

I would also like to take this opportunity to thank my own parents and my parents-in-law for their love, support and babysitting; my sister, Jane, for her encouragement and realism and my dear friend, Jocelyn, for having such a good ear and a broad shoulder to lean on.

Lastly, but by no means least, there are three very special people that I need to thank. My dear husband, Klaf, without whom I would never have survived losing Daisy, never mind had the courage and energy to write this book. And finally, Tom and Lottie, who will very sadly never know their sister, but who have made our lives worth living again.

Contents

Introduction

This book is dedicated to the memory of my beautiful daughter, Daisy, whose life was so tragically short but so infinitely sweet. Her bright red hair and her incredible smile lit up our lives but were very suddenly extinguished when she contracted a fatal infection.

Daisy became ill and died within a matter of hours – doctors couldn't fathom what might have caused an apparently healthy child to become so ill, so quickly. We later discovered that Daisy had been born with a condition called Asplenia that remained undiagnosed despite an ultrasound scan two months before her death. This basically means that she was born without a functioning spleen, resulting in a severely compromised immune system. At 10:50 a.m. on 2 April 2002, at the age of 18 months, our precious little girl died of septicaemia.

Nothing can prepare you for the death of a child, never mind a completely unexpected death like Daisy's. They say that, given time, you come to terms with it. I'm not sure that's true. I think that you learn to exist in a new world: a parallel universe where you're unfamiliar with the laws or the language. My husband and I will never come to terms with losing Daisy, we are simply inhabiting that new world and slowly learning the rules all over again.

Shortly after Daisy's death, we heard about The Isabel Medical Charity set up by Jason and Charlotte Maude, who almost lost their daughter, Isabel, to an equally rare condition. Isabel survived but Jason and Charlotte decided to create something positive out of their terrifying ordeal and, working with doctors from St. Mary's Hospital, Paddington, and wholly funded by the charity, pioneered the development of Isabel (www.isabelhealthcare.com), an on–line system that helps doctors reach an accurate diagnosis. It is a tool that might, at one time, have helped to save Daisy's life and all money raised through the sale of *Cooking with Daisy* will go to The Isabel Medical Charity, which will continue to provide funds to promote patient safety and prevent medical error.

The inspiration for this book came from the many wonderful memories that I have of Daisy in our kitchen: eating, cooking, baking for her first birthday, playing and even dancing and singing. Often it felt like we were trying to do all of these at once, but we always had fun!

So *Cooking with Daisy* is essentially a book about having fun in the kitchen, whether cooking or eating. But it doesn't ignore the fact that, if you've got a tricky eater, mealtimes aren't always fun. The first few chapters therefore concentrate on the pleasure and challenge that feeding your most precious bundles can represent. It's about creating healthy but appealing dishes that seduce their imagination as well as their palates and might even persuade the most reluctant of little eaters that mealtimes don't have to be such a drag after all. The recipes are geared towards low-effort creation, remembering that children love to get involved, and high-level appreciation. One thing that I did learn from Daisy is that there is nothing more disheartening than slavishly creating something that you consider wonderful, only for it to be thrown onto the floor when it is less well appreciated by your little darling.

In contrast, 'Pat-a-cake, pat-a-cake' focuses solely on cooking with your children. It is filled with recipes for the yummiest, sweetest and most delicious things for children to make with the help of a vaguely kitchen-friendly adult. It's all about children having fun in the kitchen, rolling up their sleeves and getting covered in flour, dough, chocolate or whatever it is that they're making. And it's about eating most of the cake mixture before it even makes it to the oven!

In short, *Cooking with Daisy* is a collection of all-time favourites, tried and tested by those preparing and those devouring. Many recipes are geared towards children with at least some teeth – think first birthday and beyond. However, the majority can be adapted for smaller siblings. In case you're not sure, each and every recipe states its age recommendation.

So, for my darling Daisy, who was and always will be my precious angel.

Since Daisy died we have become friends with other parents who have shared in our grief having lost a child of their own. They have kindly contributed to this book as well as to the maintenance of our sanity! This book is therefore also dedicated to two of Daisy's new friends:

Max Szpojnarowicz
5 May 2000 – 17 April 2002   and

Joe Gandon
25 December 2000 – 27 July 2002

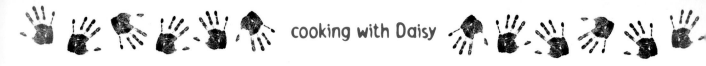

ABC to a healthy diet

Feeding your child can be an extremely happy and rewarding experience, but this is not always the case.

Many parents complain that they are bombarded with information regarding infant and child nutrition and find that the advice can be confusing and, in many cases, conflicting and misleading. But the truth is that ensuring optimal nutrition for your child is actually very simple.

Here are the basic rules. It is important that your child receives three balanced meals, with or without snacks inbetween, every day. The simplest way to ensure that a meal is nutritionally complete is to use 'the plate model'.

Protein
Essential for growth and a good source of iron. Good sources include: any meat, chicken, fish, cheese, baked beans, lentils, eggs, yogurt, tofu and milk.

At least one vegetable or fruit
Provide essential vitamins and minerals for normal growth and development.

Carbohydrate (starch)
Provides the child with energy. Sources include: bread, pasta, rice, potatoes, corn, breakfast cereals, porridge.

Protein and carbohydrate sources are pretty straightforward but you can get bogged down when it comes to working out which essential vitamins and minerals are contained in which fruit and vegetables. The key is to provide a variety of fruit and vegetables and, in doing so, you automatically ensure that your child gets all the vitamins and minerals they need.

Sounds easy? On paper it is, but every parent knows that children will not always eat every piece of fruit or every vegetable that comes their way. If your child protests when it comes to eating greens, be creative, try hiding or disguising them as many of the recipes suggest.

If this all sounds too worthy and idealistic, don't panic! The good news is that treats don't need to be outlawed to achieve a healthy diet. As adults, we are constantly bombarded with reminders that we should follow a healthy low-fat regime but it is not necessary for a healthy child to be restricted in this way. Of course it's important to limit snacks that are high in sugar (sweets, chocolates and many juices) and salt (crisps) but you don't need to cut them out altogether. Present them as occasional rather than everyday snacks and try to encourage more regular snacking on foods like fruit, yogurt or homemade smoothies.

Finally, try to ensure that mealtimes are a relaxed and pleasurable time for all and encourage your child to get involved in the preparation of their meals to create an all-round more engaging experience.

Sample Menus

Sample Menu 1

Breakfast	Protein	Carbohydrate	Fruit or Vegetable
Mummy's Muffins	✔	✔	
Glass of fruit juice			✔

Lunch	Protein	Carbohydrate	Fruit or Vegetable
Granny's Bolognaise	✔		
Baked potato		✔	
1 Banana			✔

Tea/Dinner	Protein	Carbohydrate	Fruit or Vegetable
Easy Cheesy Macaroni	✔	✔	
Steamed broccoli			✔

Sample Menu 2

Breakfast	Protein	Carbohydrate	Fruit or Vegetable
My Favourite Healthy Breakfast	✔	✔	✔

Lunch	Protein	Carbohydrate	Fruit or Vegetable
Toad in the Hole	✔	✔	
1 Apple			✔

Tea/Dinner	Protein	Carbohydrate	Fruit or Vegetable
Louis's Stir-Fry	✔		✔
Noodles or rice		✔	

Sample Menu 3

Breakfast	Protein	Carbohydrate	Fruit or Vegetable
Ricotta Hotcakes	✔	✔	
Strawberries			✔

Lunch	Protein	Carbohydrate	Fruit or Vegetable
Griddled Salmon	✔		
Griddled or mashed potato		✔	
Smiley Oranges			✔

Tea/Dinner	Protein	Carbohydrate	Fruit or Vegetable
All-Round Ratatouille			✔
Bread (any)		✔	
Grated cheese	✔		

Practical and nutritional information

The symbols at the beginning of each recipe answer all of those practical questions that spring to mind when you contemplate what to cook: How long will it take me to make this? How many people will it serve? Is it suitable for the entire family? Can I freeze any leftovers? The answers to these questions are contained in a key at the top of every recipe that aims to give you an 'at a glance' view as to whether your chosen recipe really suits your needs:

Some recipes are what I would consider to be staple family meals. They're great because it means that you can make enough to feed you and your partner later that day and all of your cooking is done in one fell swoop. Others are very much designed with kids in mind and are perhaps slightly less sophisticated in flavour or, otherwise, just more fun to eat. It's useful to know which is which before you start, then you know how much to make.

As a mother, I love to have a freezer full of homemade ready meals for busy or lazy days. For that reason, I always want to know whether I should make more than I need so that I can freeze batches for another day. Every recipe tells you whether it's suitable for freezing or not, so that you can decide how much to make in one go.

However many kids you have, there are bound to be days when you are feeding other people's too. The aim here is to give you a ready-reckoner when planning and buying ingredients. Portion sizes are obviously approximations since children's appetites vary enormously. I've also tried to allow for adult portions with some of the family food.

If you've got more than one child, you'll want to get them all eating the same thing as soon as is practically possible, if only to save yourself from becoming a slave to the kitchen. So many of these recipes are suitable from 8 months and can be puréed to whatever consistency your youngest desires. Some can even be given to infants from 6 months. Each recipe tells you at what age your children should be happy eating it.

How long does it take to make? For me this is the key to decision-making when it comes to considering a recipe. Remember that almost all of these recipes, with the odd exception, are geared towards low-effort creation, so you're not going to find anything too complex or time-consuming. That said, they do vary from the, 'It's-quarter-to-five-and-I've-nothing-to-feed-the-children-for-tea' type of scramble to those that require slightly more thought and planning. Each recipe tells you exactly how much time you need from raw ingredients to plate on table and, where appropriate, recipes also indicate how much of this time is taken up in preparation (bowl symbol) and, how much time you can, in theory, put your feet up for while it's cooking (oven symbol).

The nutritional guide, on the other hand, gives you an easy-to-digest summary of what you'll actually be feeding your child, together with other useful information.

This book contains occasional tips for parents of children who suffer from food allergies. However, it does not attempt to give comprehensive advice for any category of food allergy sufferer. If you or your child suffer from a food-related allergy always be sure to check the suitability of every ingredient and read all packaging carefully. If you have concerns, always consult your GP or a dietitian.

Conversion tables

You will find that different recipe books offer slightly different versions of this metric/imperial conversion chart. Don't be put off by this, the difference of a few grams here or half an ounce there generally isn't going to lead to instant culinary disaster. All of the recipes in this book have already been converted to make life easy for you but here's a ready-reckoner in case you need it.

Weight	
Metric	**Imperial**
10 g	¼ oz
15 g	½ oz
25/30 g	1 oz
35 g	1¼ oz
40 g	1½ oz
50/55 g	2 oz
75/85 g	3 oz
100 g	3½ oz
115 g	4 oz
125 g	4½ oz
140 g	5 oz
150 g	5½ oz
175 g	6 oz
200 g	7 oz
225 g	8 oz
250 g	9 oz
275 g	9¾ oz
280 g	10 oz
300 g	10½ oz
325 g	11½ oz
350 g	12 oz
375 g	13 oz
400 g	14 oz
425 g	15 oz
450 g	1 lb

Volume	
Metric	**Imperial**
5 ml	½ fl oz
30 ml	1 fl oz
50 ml	2 fl oz
75 ml	2½ fl oz
100 ml	3½ fl oz
125 ml	4 fl oz
150 ml	5 fl oz/¼ pint
175 ml	6 fl oz
200 ml	7 fl oz/⅓ pint
225 ml	8 fl oz
250 ml	9 fl oz
300 ml	10 fl oz/½ pint
350 ml	12 fl oz
400 ml	14 fl oz
425 ml	15 fl oz/¾ pint
450 ml	16 fl oz
500 ml	18 fl oz
568 ml	1 pint milk
600 ml	20 fl oz/1 pint
700 ml	1¼ pints
850 ml	1½ pints
1 litre	1¾ pints
1.2 litres	2 pints

1

who's been eating my porridge?

Tasty ideas for breakfast

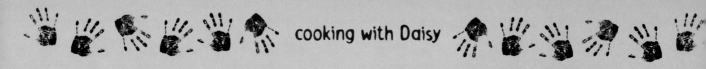
Fruit Smoothies

 Kid's food   Do not freeze   2 kids   12 months   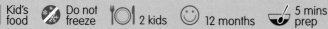 5 mins prep

Children love making smoothies and while it's a great way of getting them to drink enough milk, it also provides a good disguise for dull old fruit! Here is a recipe for a basic smoothie that you can adapt to any number of flavours.

150 ml (5 fl oz) whole milk
85 g (3 oz) natural yogurt
1 dessertspoon honey

And to flavour, one of the following:

1 banana
85 g (3 oz) raspberries
85 g (3 oz) strawberries
85 g (3 oz) crumbled chocolate biscuits

1. Put all of the ingredients and your chosen fruit (or, for a treat, crumbled chocolate biscuits) into the blender and whiz for about 1 minute or until it is evenly mixed and creamy.

2. Pour into a tall glass, add a couple of straws and it's ready for drinking.

Sheila Harris, Granny to Rachel, Andrew and Matthew

NUTRITIONAL INFORMATION • Smoothies provide an excellent way of disguising fruit. Try to use live natural yogurts, which contain healthy live bacteria. If your child has difficulty gaining weight, you can add 1–2 tablespoons of double cream.

Of course, you won't always have suitable fresh fruit hanging around but here's a great idea for instant smoothies made with pre-frozen fruit. It was sent to me by a friend who used to live in the much sunnier climes of Southern Spain where she grew her own strawberries and constantly had too many to know what to do with them. It's perfect if you've got any suitable fruit that is about to go off and just can't all be eaten that day.

strawberries or other freezable fruit (blueberries, blackberries, raspberries and over-ripe pears all freeze well and make great smoothies)
fresh fruit juice
your child's preferred milk

1. Blitz the fruit with a dash of milk in the blender and then freeze the mixture in ice cube trays. Once frozen, press them out and freeze them in plastic freezer bags, just as you would with baby purées.

2. They can then be made into quick and easy smoothies throughout the year. Simply pour half a glass of whatever fruit juice you have open in the fridge (peach juice makes lovely rich smoothies and apple works really well too), top up with milk and then pop in three or four fruit ice cubes and a sprig of fresh mint if you've got it. As the ice cubes melt you'll be left with a delicious fruit smoothie.

Since these cheat's smoothies don't contain honey, they can be given to infants from 6 months.

Bee Trim, Mummy to Jasper and Rohanna

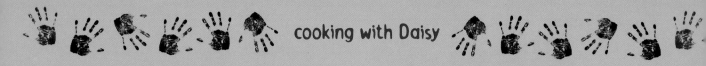

Going Along Eggs (or Eggy Bread)

Family food | Do not freeze | 3–4 kids | 8 months | 5-10 mins total

I was sent more than one recipe for Eggy Bread or French Toast, as some people call it. However, this one particularly caught my eye because of the name. According to the father who sent it to me, his father used to make it for him as a boy when they were holidaying on canal boats. It was the one thing that his father could make, albeit he couldn't cook, and because it could be made while the boat was moving, the dish was given the name 'Going Along Eggs'.

1–2 eggs (depending on their size)
whole milk
3–4 slices white bread
butter

1. Beat the eggs together with a splash of milk. Pour them onto a flat plate and soak the slices of bread, one at a time, until both sides have soaked up a fair amount of egg and are fully coated.

2. Warm some butter in a non-stick frying pan and fry each slice of 'eggy bread' on both sides until golden brown.

For a sweet tooth, serve with maple or golden syrup or simply sprinkled with caster sugar. For a savoury version try eggy bread soldiers dunked in ketchup; sliced with Marmite on top or as eggy bacon sandwiches.

Becky and Mark Rubens, parents to Isabel, Tabitha and Gabriel

NUTRITIONAL INFORMATION
Eggy bread can be served as breakfast or a light meal. It contains both carbohydrate (bread) and protein (egg). Combine it with diluted fruit juice or a piece of fruit for a complete meal for the growing child.

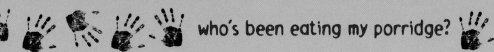 

Mummy's Muffins

 Family food | Do not freeze | 3 kids | 12 months | 10 mins total

Muffins make a great breakfast but there's no reason why they couldn't be revisited for a delicious and quick lunch or tea. This recipe makes as good a muffin as you can buy anywhere.

6 slices white bread
3 eggs
3 slices Cheddar cheese
butter
bacon or ham (optional)

1. Butter both sides of the bread slices and use a circular biscuit cutter to make a hole in the middle of three of them, creating a 'nest' for the egg. Kids will love making the holes themselves.

2. Place the buttered, holed bread into a frying pan on a gentle heat. Put a small knob of butter in the hole and when the butter melts crack an egg into the 'nest'.

3. When the egg white starts to turn white, cover it with a slice of Cheddar and top that with another piece of buttered bread (intact). Turn over until brown on both sides.

Pre-grilled bacon or cooked ham can be added before the last slice of bread if desired. Serve sunny-side-up!

Maxine Leslau, Mummy to Ori, Jake and Jonah

NUTRITIONAL INFORMATION

An ideal breakfast for children and an excellent source of protein (egg, cheese & bacon/ham), and iron. The bread adds the carbohydrate source, so all it needs is a piece of fruit or diluted fruit juice.

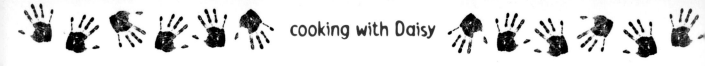

American Pancakes

 Family food ❄ Do not freeze 🍽 3–6 kids ☺ 8 months 🥄 10 mins prep ▭ 10 mins cooking

A recipe that is ideal for children who get lots of exercise during the day and need plenty of energy, this mixture makes roughly 24 small pancakes and, according to the mother that sent it to me, her son, Tom, can manage up to 8 in one sitting!

30 g (1 oz) unsalted butter
225 g (8 oz) plain flour
2 heaped tsp baking powder
1 tsp sugar
300 ml (½ pint) whole milk
2 eggs
salt (optional)

1. Melt the butter in a pan or in the microwave and then combine this with all of the other ingredients and a pinch of salt, if desired, in a blender. Mix until smooth and really well combined. Technically, pancake batter should be left to stand for sometime before cooking; you can make it the night before and leave it in the fridge overnight. Otherwise, try to leave it for half an hour if you have time. If you don't, don't worry.

2. Heat another knob of butter in a shallow frying pan and then fry the batter in 5–6 cm (2–2½ inch) rounds on both sides until golden brown. Use a palate knife or fish slice to turn them.

Serve with maple syrup or add chopped fruit for a healthy option. These can also be served with ice cream for a yummy pudding.

Jo Perkins, Mummy to Kate and Tom

NUTRITIONAL INFORMATION
These pancakes are a great source of carbohydrate. Create a complete meal by adding chopped fruit with mascarpone cheese (protein), or serve with maple syrup and fruit, followed by yogurt.

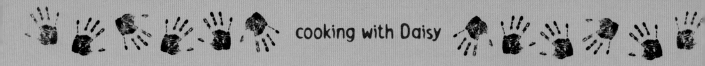
Ricotta Hotcakes

 Family food   **Do not freeze**   **2 adults + 2–3 kids**   **8 months**   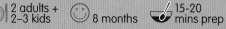 **15-20 mins prep**   **10 mins cooking**

If you're looking for a variation on a regular American pancake, try these. Children will love the mixing and whipping up of the egg whites into soft peaks with an electric whisk.

They are great eaten with maple syrup, golden syrup or honey but they are also delicious with fruit – blueberries, strawberries or sliced banana for example. For a savoury option, try them with bacon and scrambled egg (with maple syrup drizzling deliciously onto the bacon). They are great for Sunday mornings when breakfast can be late and tends to become brunch.

This version is based on a recipe from *Sydney Food*, by Bill Grainger.

300 g (10 oz) ricotta cheese
180 ml (6 fl oz) whole milk
4 eggs, separated
175 g (6 oz) plain flour
1 tsp baking powder
salt (optional)
butter, for cooking

1. Put the ricotta, milk and egg yolks in a bowl and mix.

2. In another bowl, sift the flour, then add the baking power and a pinch of salt. Mix with the ricotta mixture.

3. Put the egg whites in a dry, clean bowl and whisk (with an electric hand-whisk) until they make lovely white soft peaks, and slip cleanly from a metal spoon. Fold them into the batter with the metal spoon.

NUTRITIONAL INFORMATION
Ricotta hotcakes are extremely nutritious. Ricotta cheese, although high in fat, is a good protein source (if your child has proven excessive weight gain, avoid a high-fat breakfast). Serving the hotcakes with fruit makes it a complete and nutritious breakfast.

4. To cook, heat a little butter in a heavy non-stick frying pan until it's medium hot. To make large-ish hotcakes, drop two spoonfuls of the batter per hotcake into the pan, you can make them smaller if you prefer. Depending on how large your pan is, cook between 2 and 4 at a time, but don't let them run into each other, the batter should be firm enough to make them hold their shape. Cook on a medium to low heat for about 2 minutes each side, until they are golden brown. Add more butter between batches if necessary. Serve as you fancy.

The hotcakes are best just cooked as they maintain a slightly crisp surface; you can cook them a bit in advance and keep them in a warm oven but they do go a bit soggy.

Miranda Carter, Mummy to Finn and Jesse

who's been eating my porridge?

My Favourite Healthy Breakfast

👪 Kid's food   ⊘ Do not freeze   ☺ 8 months   🥣 2 mins prep

So called because it uses your child's favourite fruit and favourite breakfast cereal, giving a perfectly balanced start to the day. It also makes a great pudding, particularly if the first course didn't go down so well.

favourite fruit (banana, grapes and strawberries work very well)
favourite cereal (Rice Crispies, Cheerios etc.)
1 dessertspoon natural yogurt

Chop the fruit into bowls, spoon on a little yogurt and sprinkle generously with cereal.

Couldn't be easier.

Zoe Brent, Mummy to Jordan and Leah

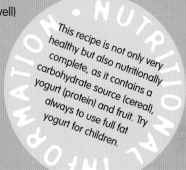

NUTRITIONAL INFORMATION • This recipe is not only very healthy but also nutritionally complete, as it contains a carbohydrate source (cereal), yogurt (protein) and fruit. Try always to use full fat yogurt for children.

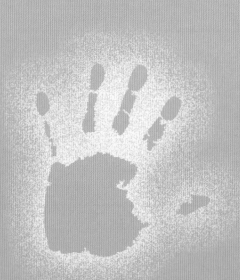

Breakfast Baskets

 Family food   Do not freeze   4 kids   12 months   20 mins total

The broadcaster and presenter, Emma Forbes, kindly donated this recipe. These look great and provide a fairly hearty family breakfast for an action-packed day.

4 slices brown or white bread
butter
4 eggs
2 tbsp whole milk
salt and pepper (if desired)
2 small tomatoes
50 g (2 oz) grated Cheddar cheese

1. Preheat the oven to 200°C (fan 180°C), 400°F or Gas Mark 6, then cut the crusts off the bread and spread both sides with butter (this can get a little sticky). Press each slice into a muffin tin. Place in the oven for about 10 minutes, or until they look golden and crisp.

2. While they are in the oven, melt a little butter in a saucepan over a low heat. Whisk together the eggs, milk and a little salt and pepper in a bowl. Pour into the melted butter and scramble over a low heat, stirring constantly with a spatula (I find the best thing for scrambled eggs is a rubber spatula that allows you to get all of the cooked egg off the sides and bottom of the pan) until done to your liking.

3. Place the toast baskets on a heatproof plate and divide the egg mixture evenly between them. Add half a tomato to each one (flat side down), and sprinkle a little grated cheese over the top. Place under a hot grill (not too close to the grill or the baskets will burn) for about 5 minutes until bubbling.

Toothless wonders might enjoy cheesy, eggy scramble with some softer buttered bread.

NUTRITIONAL INFORMATION • Breakfast is the most important meal for a growing child. This recipe is nutritionally complete, with a good source of carbohydrate (bread), protein (egg and cheese) and tomato.

2

hickety pickety, my black hen

Chicken dishes

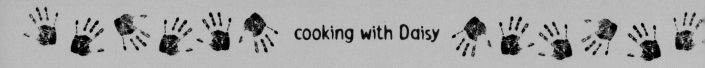

    cooking with Daisy

Honey and Mustard Chicken

| 👪 Family food | ❄ Do not freeze | 🍴 2–4 kids | 😊 12 months | 🥄 10 mins prep 2 hrs marinating | 📺 15–20 mins cooking |

Children will love these delicious chicken pieces and they are so easy to prepare as long as you start with enough time to let them marinate. The flavour is beautifully sweet and since they can be eaten with fingers, they are bound to be a hit.

4 chicken thighs, skinless
4 tbsp lemon juice
1 tbsp vegetable oil
4 tbsp clear honey
2 tbsp wholegrain mustard
2.5 cm (1 inch) fresh ginger, grated
1 red chilli, seeds removed, chopped
2 tbsp chopped fresh coriander to serve

1. Slash the chicken thighs with a sharp knife and put them in a flat bowl.

2. Mix the lemon juice with the vegetable oil, honey, mustard, ginger, and red chilli – spoon over the chicken, making sure that each piece is coated with the mixture. Cover the bowl and set aside for around 2 hours or so.

3. Remove the chicken pieces from the marinade, and cook under a hot grill until the honey caramelises and the chicken is tender – about 8–10 minutes on each side. Drizzle a spoon or so of the marinade over the chicken as it cooks to help keep it succulent.

Serve hot, scattered with fresh coriander and accompanied with a bowl of hot steamy rice or oven chips if you really want to earn brownie points. If your child is not ready to cope with gnawing round a bone, simply remove the meat from the bone before serving.

A huge thank you to Roopa Gulati for this recipe

NUTRITIONAL INFORMATION
Chicken is a very good source of protein and iron. This easy-to-eat recipe also introduces several new flavours, including tasty spices. It's always a great idea to introduce new flavours early on as this helps to broaden a child's repertoire and to avoid fussy eating later.

Balti Chicken

 Family food • Do not freeze •   2 adults + 3–4 kids • ☺ 8 months • 🥄+📺 35 mins total

This has a delicious mildly spiced, creamy texture and is perfect for the entire family. Don't be put off by the longish list of herbs and spices, it's actually incredibly simple and quick to make. But if you don't have them all, or you are looking for simplicity, substitute the 5 individual herbs and spices with 1-2 tablespoons of mild curry powder.

4 boneless, skinless chicken breasts, chopped into small pieces
1 onion, finely chopped
2 courgettes, sliced
3 tbsp vegetable oil
1 tsp ground coriander
1 tsp ground cumin
1 tsp ground ginger
1 tsp turmeric
½ tsp chilli powder
230 g can chopped tomatoes
1 tsp sugar
142 ml (4½ fl oz) pot soured cream
50 g (2 oz) creamed coconut, chopped
salt and pepper, if desired

NUTRITIONAL INFORMATION: This is an excellent combination of protein and vegetables. It will also expose your child to different and more unusual flavours, something to be encouraged from an early age. Serve with rice for a wholesome and complete meal.

1. Prepare the chicken breasts, onion and courgettes and then heat a tablespoon of the oil in a large pan and fry the onion until soft. Stir in all of the herbs and spices (or 2 tablespoons of curry powder) and cook for 1 minute.

2. Add the sliced courgettes, tomatoes and sugar, bring to the boil and simmer for 10 minutes.

3. While this curry sauce is cooking, heat the remaining oil in a wok or large frying pan and stir-fry the chicken in batches until all the pieces are golden brown.

4. Add the chicken to the curry sauce along with the soured cream and the creamed coconut. Bring it to the boil once again, stirring all the time, and cook until the creamed coconut has completely dissolved. Season to taste if you wish and serve immediately with basmati rice.

Marie-Christine Willis, Mummy to Alexandra, Catalina and Matthew

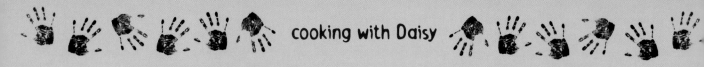
Stuff that Chicken!

 Family food   Do not freeze   1–2 kids   12 months   10 mins prep  25 mins cooking

A great idea for chicken breasts from Katie Caldesi, who, along with her husband, Giancarlo, owns and runs Caffé Caldesi in London's Marylebone Lane. Her children adore the preparation as much as the eating since it involves bashing out the breast before stuffing it.

1 chicken breast
3–4 slices mozzarella
1 slice prosciutto or cooked ham
olive oil for frying

Preheat your oven to 180°C (fan 160°C), 350°F or Gas Mark 4.

Split the chicken breast in half sideways and open it out. Cover it with a layer of clingfilm and flatten it a little with a wooden mallet or something similar.

Lay a piece of ham over the chicken and then place some slices of mozzarella on top of that. Fold it in half and secure it with 2 or 3 toothpicks to keep it closed. Sprinkle with a little salt if desired.

Fry the chicken breast on both sides in hot oil in a frying pan until golden brown and then transfer to an ovenproof dish and bake for 25 minutes or until the meat juices run clear when pierced with a sharp knife.

Cut into slices or chop up for younger children and serve. Delicious with broccoli and cheesy mash that you can make by stirring grated Parmesan and a little olive oil into mashed potato. If your children like garlic, you can always spread a little garlic butter over the chicken before stuffing it.

Katie Caldesi, Mummy to Giorgio and Flavio

NUTRITIONAL INFORMATION • This chicken recipe is packed with protein since it also contains ham and cheese. It's ideal for a day when you have struggled to get a child to eat the protein constituent of other meals.

Swiss Chicken

👨‍👩‍👧 Family food ❄ Do not freeze 🍽 2 adults + 2–4 kids ☺ 8 months 🥄 10 mins prep 📟 30-40 mins cooking

This is a wonderfully simple recipe that goes down well time and time again. The best thing about it is that the base for the sauce is a couple of cans of soup and so it couldn't be easier to make. It can be puréed for toothless wonders but please note that the soup does contain salt so it's advisable to make it an occasional rather than everyday meal for the youngest members of the family.

4 boneless, skinless chicken breasts
enough broccoli to cover the bottom of an ovenproof dish, roughly 28 x 18 cm (11 x 7 inches), or other vegetable of your choice, leeks and asparagus work well
1 tbsp mayonnaise
1 tbsp double cream
2 tbsp lemon juice
1 tsp curry powder
150 ml (¼ pint) whole milk
2 x 295 g cans Campbell's condensed chicken or mushroom soup
handful of grated cheese (around 75 g/3 oz)
handful of breadcrumbs (around 75 g/3 oz)
handful of crushed cornflakes (around 50 g/2 oz)

NUTRITIONAL INFORMATION • This is an excellent dish combining a vegetable and chicken, a great protein source. It is particularly energy-dense and therefore good for children with small appetites.

1. Preheat the oven to 180°C (fan 160°C), 350°F or Gas Mark 4 and prepare the broccoli (or vegetable of your choice) by parboiling or lightly steaming. Don't overcook at this stage since it will all go in the oven later. Cover the bottom of your ovenproof dish with the broccoli.

2. Cut your chicken breasts into bite-sized chunks. You can do this with chicken leftovers as well as breasts and it can be a really good way of using up the remainder of a Sunday roast (cut the cooking time down to around 20–25 minutes if using pre-cooked chicken). Lay the chicken pieces over the broccoli.

3. Combine the mayonnaise, double cream, lemon juice, curry powder, milk and soup and pour the sauce over the chicken and vegetable pieces.

4. The topping is as simple to make as the sauce. Combine the cheese, breadcrumbs and crushed cornflakes and cover the entire dish. This will make a wonderfully crisp topping. Bake for 30–40 minutes until the chicken pieces are cooked through and the topping is bubbling, crispy and golden brown. Serve with rice or potatoes.

Chloe Barker, Mummy to Joe and Ella

Louis's Chicken Stir-Fry

 Family food   Do not freeze    3–4 kids   ☺ 12 months   25 mins total

This recipe was created by a friend of mine who needed a quick, nourishing meal to serve to her two boys after a long and tiring winter walk. It was such a hit with her 2-year-old, Louis, that he rifled through the trough at the bottom of his bib looking for leftovers when it was all gone.

You will need a wok or deep-sided frying pan with a lid.

2 boneless, skinless chicken breasts, finely chopped
1 clove garlic, peeled and finely chopped
2.5cm (1 inch) fresh ginger, peeled and finely chopped
50 g (2 oz) broccoli, chopped
50 g (2 oz) French beans, chopped
soy sauce
2 tbsp honey
vegetable oil for cooking

NUTRITION INFORMATION A stir-fry is a quick and easy meal that provides a protein as well as vegetables. This recipe is also a great way to introduce new flavours such as ginger and garlic into a child's diet. Remember to serve with noodles or rice to make this dish a complete meal.

1. Heat some oil in your wok and gently cook the garlic and ginger for about 5 minutes.

2. Add the chicken and stir-fry on a medium heat until it has browned.

3. Add the broccoli, beans and a little soy sauce along with a splash of water. Cover the wok and leave it to cook through for about 8 minutes.

4. Stir in the honey and add salt and pepper to taste if you wish.

Serve with noodles or rice.

Lisa Hynes, Mummy to Milo, Louis and Lara

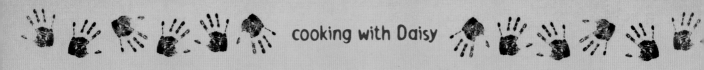

Roast Chicken with Fennel

Family food | Do not freeze | 2 adults + 3–4 kids | 12 months | 25-30 mins prep | 40 mins cooking

I think that roast chicken and fennel make one of the most delicious culinary combinations. You might dismiss it as a dish for children but it's a great idea to get kids to try unusual flavours like fennel when they are young and before they've made up their minds that they aren't going to like anything new. This is a dish for the entire family and it's incredibly simple to make.

8–12 chicken joints, leaving the skin on and bones intact for flavour
300 g (10 oz) shallots, peeled
3 tbsp olive oil
2 large or 3 medium fennel bulbs
300 ml (10 fl oz) homemade stock (see page 82), or use a good alternative such as Marigold Swiss Vegetable Bouillon Powder
few sprigs fresh thyme
2–3 bay leaves
75 g (3 oz) freshly grated Parmesan cheese
salt and pepper, if desired

1. Preheat the oven to 200°C (fan 180°C), 400°F or Gas Mark 6.

2. Place the chicken and shallots in a roasting tin, coat them well in the olive oil and season with salt and pepper if desired. Roast them uncovered for 20 minutes.

3. While they are roasting, cut the fennel into wedges and pop them into a pan of boiling water for just 2–3 minutes to soften them slightly. Drain them well and, once the chicken has been cooking for 20 minutes, add the fennel (if you are short of time, you can throw the uncooked fennel wedges in with the chicken and shallots right at the start). Toss the chicken, fennel and shallots together to ensure that they are all re-coated in oil. Pour in the stock and tuck in the thyme and bay leaves.

NUTRITIONAL INFORMATION: Not only does this dish introduce children to a new and unusual flavour – the younger you introduce new ingredients, the more adventurous they will become – but it also provides an excellent source of protein in the chicken.

4. Return the roasting tin to the oven, uncovered, and cook for a further 30 minutes, basting 2–3 times. By now, the stock should have almost evaporated and the chicken should be cooked.

5. Sprinkle the grated Parmesan over the fennel and chicken pieces, baste the whole lot one more time, and return to the oven for 5–10 minutes until the Parmesan starts to brown.

This should be served immediately and is great with roast potatoes, rice or chunks of warm bread.

If you are serving this to younger children and are concerned about the bones in the chicken, simply remove the meat from the bones before serving. It really is a one-pot roast for the whole family.

Sophie Scobie, Mummy to Charlotte and Tilly

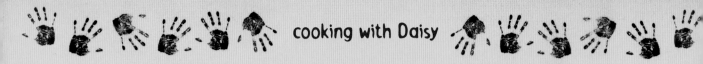

cooking with Daisy

Chicken Veggie Balls

Kid's food · Can be frozen · 3–4 kids · 12 months · 10 mins prep · 10–20 mins cooking

If you are freezing these be sure to use fresh chicken, not chicken that has already been frozen and thawed.

2 boneless, skinless chicken breasts
1 leek, 1 carrot, 1 small onion
mixed herbs
2 slices white bread, crusts off and roughly chunked
1 tbsp Marigold Swiss Vegetable Bouillon Powder
1 egg
vegetable oil for cooking
plain flour

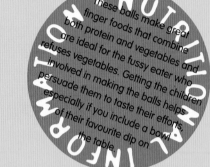

NUTRITIONAL INFORMATION

These balls make great finger foods that combine both protein and vegetables and are ideal for the fussy eater who refuses vegetables. Getting the children involved in making the balls helps persuade them to taste their efforts, especially if you include a bowl of their favourite dip on the table.

1. Peel and prepare the vegetables, chopping them fairly roughly. Then roughly chop the chicken. Place the vegetables and chicken in a food processor and add a pinch of herbs, bread, the stock powder and the beaten egg. Blend until fairly smooth.

2. Then use your hands to make little balls. Make sure hands are washed and get kids involved here – it's fairly sticky and good fun. Coat the balls with flour and then shallow fry them in hot oil for about 8–10 minutes or until they are golden brown. Serve them with ketchup, mashed potato or chips and sneak in another vegetable if you can.

Victoria Maby, Mummy to Oliver, Louisa and Freddie

Homemade Chicken Nuggets

Kid's food · Do not freeze · 2–4 kids · 12 months · 10-15 mins prep · 10 mins cooking

Chicken nuggets are always a hit. By making your own, you can ensure that the best quality chicken is used.

2 chicken breasts
2 slices of white bread, blitzed into breadcrumbs
2 egg yolks
Worcestershire sauce

NUTRITIONAL INFORMATION

Use good quality chicken breasts to make them, and grill rather than fry. These are an excellent protein source and also a fantastic finger food that can be dipped into any number of things including ketchup, guacamole (for the adventurous child) and cream cheese (for the child with poor weight gain).

1. Cut the chicken into nugget-sized chunks. Mix the egg yolks in a bowl with a few drops of water and a few drops of Worcestershire sauce.

2. Stir the chicken pieces into the egg yolk and drop them one at a time into the breadcrumbs, coating them well

3. Cook them on a baking tray under a hot grill, turning them until they are golden brown on both sides. Cooking time should be around 10 minutes (5 minutes on each side), depending on the size of your nuggets. To ensure they are cooked through, cut one in half and make sure that the flesh is white throughout. Serve with ketchup, of course!

Phillipa Hawkins, Mummy to Cara

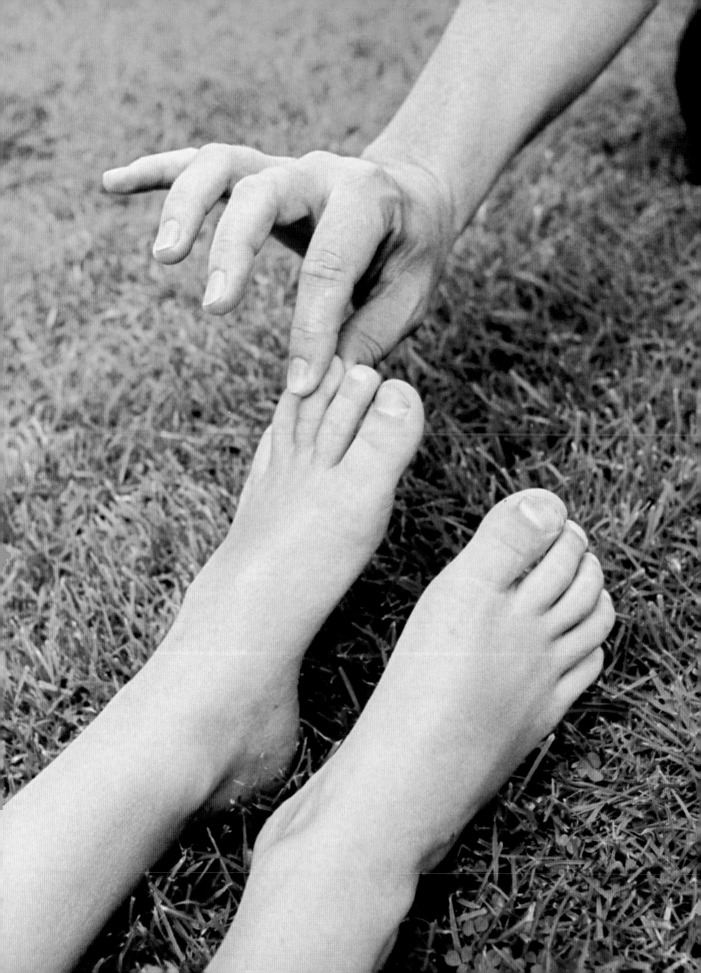

3

this little piggy had roast beef

Meat dishes

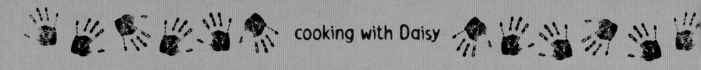

Yeaton Sausage Casserole

Family food | Freezes well | 2 adults + 3–4 kids | 18 months | 25–30 mins prep | 25–30 mins cooking

Most children, from toddlers to teenagers, will eat and enjoy sausages and this is the ideal dish if you've got a houseful of kids, hence the fairly hefty quantities. It's a very quick and easy way to prepare them in a slightly different guise with vegetables thrown in.

You don't need to worry about the wine in this recipe; during cooking all the alcohol disappears and you are simply left with the flavour. However, feel free to leave it out and use slightly more stock to compensate if necessary.

900 g (2 lb) pork sausages
4 medium onions, thinly sliced
1 tsp fresh thyme (use ½ tsp dried if you can't get fresh)
6 carrots, peeled and sliced
6 sticks celery, sliced
1 tbsp plain flour
1 tbsp oil
150 ml (¼ pint) red wine
300 ml (½ pint) homemade stock (see page 82), or a good alternative
    such as a Marigold Swiss Vegetable Bouillon Powder
salt and pepper if desired

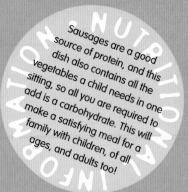

NUTRITIONAL INFORMATION
Sausages are a good source of protein, and this dish also contains all the vegetables a child needs in one sitting, so all you are required to add is a carbohydrate. This will make a satisfying meal for a family with children, of all ages, and adults too!

1. Prepare the vegetables and set them to one side.

2. Heat the oil in a large saucepan and cook the sausages for 5–10 minutes, turning frequently until browned. Remove the sausages from the pan and set aside.

3. Add the onions and thyme to the same saucepan and stir-fry for around 5 minutes until browned. Add the carrots and the celery and continue to stir-fry for a further 3–4 minutes.

4. Sprinkle the flour into the pan and cook for 2–3 minutes, stirring frequently, until browned. Pour in the wine and stock and stir continuously until smooth, then bring to the boil stirring until slightly thickened. Return the sausages to the pan, season and return to the boil.

5. Turn the heat right down, cover and simmer very gently for 25–30 minutes until the vegetables are tender and the sausages are cooked through.

Serve with baked or mashed potatoes.

Fenella Davies, Mummy to Sam, Alice and William

Granny's Bolognaise

 Family food   Freezes well   2 adults + 2–3 kids   ☺ 8 months   🥄+🍴 40–45 mins total

This is one of my mother's basic staples. As she points out, when we were young children, this would have been referred to as 'mince' but thirty years later and with slightly more of a European influence in our kitchens, our children, and her grandchildren, know it as bolognaise.

That doesn't necessarily dictate that it has to be served with pasta. This basic recipe can be adapted and served up in various different guises so don't be afraid to make more than you need – it can be stored in the fridge or freezer to provide ready meals for a busy day.

450 g (1 lb) minced beef (or lamb if you prefer)
1 onion, finely chopped
2 carrots, finely chopped
400 g can chopped tomatoes
2 tbsp tomato purée
150 ml (¼ pint) red wine (or water, if you prefer)
olive oil for cooking
salt and pepper, if desired

1. Take a large flat-based pan or high-sided frying pan and brown the onions in a little olive oil.

2. Add the minced beef and stir-fry until browned. Add the carrot and continue to stir-fry for a further 3–5 minutes.

3. Add the tomatoes, wine (or water) and tomato purée, mix well and season if you wish. Cover the pan and simmer for 25–30 minutes.

You can either serve this immediately or divide it up and store it as you wish. My mother serves it for her grandchildren with either pasta or mashed or baked potatoes. Personally, I love it with mash. It can easily be blended for toothless wonders and is suitable for all meat-eaters over eight months. You can vary the basic recipe by adding mushrooms, baked beans, diced bacon or whatever you like, depending on your child's current fad.

Susan Smith, Granny to George, Daisy, Edward, Tom and Lottie

NUTRITIONAL INFORMATION
Bolognaise has excellent nutritional value. Mince is an outstanding source of protein and iron, and both tomato ingredients are good vitamin C sources. Add 1–2 tablespoons double cream if your child is not keeping up with his/her growth chart. Use water instead of wine for children under 12 months.

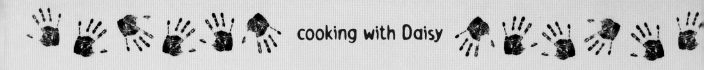
Toad in the Hole

 Family food   Do not freeze   2 adults + 2–4 kids   12 months  20 mins prep 30 mins chilling   40 mins cooking

Toad in the Hole is basically Yorkshire pudding with sausages in it, for those who have never heard of it. My mother was born and bought up in Yorkshire so Yorkshire pudding, with or without the sausages, was a staple in our house. They are the yummiest comfort food known to man and no child should be denied the odd Yorkshire now and again. Toad in the Hole served with a vegetable is a complete meal but Yorkshires are also delicious served on their own with a little gravy; with roast beef, of course; or, if you're really lucky, with golden syrup for pudding.

8 of your favourite sausages
115 g (4 oz) self-raising flour
1 egg, beaten
300 ml (½ pint) whole milk
30g (1 oz) dripping or lard, or a little vegetable oil if you prefer
salt

1. Sift the flour and a pinch of salt into a mixing bowl. Make a well in the centre and pour in the beaten egg and the milk. Using a hand whisk, gradually draw the flour into the liquid from the sides, continuing until the batter is smooth and of a pouring consistency. Chill in the fridge for 30 minutes to 1 hour.

2. While the batter stands in the fridge, you need to brown your sausages in a little oil in a frying pan. Use around 8 sausages for this amount of batter. If you have children of different ages, you can adapt this dish by using different kinds of sausages. Use grown-up sausages for those who can cope with them and then save a corner of the dish for small, skinless sausages for those who are still waiting for their real sausage-eating gnashers to grow. Anybody can, and most probably will, eat the Yorkshire pudding bit so you have an age-adaptable lunch or supper all in one dish.

3. As you cook the sausages, preheat the oven to 220°C (fan 200°C), 425°F or Gas Mark 7. When the batter is ready, put the fat (or oil) into a roasting tin (about 28 x 18 cm/11 x 7 inches) and place it in the oven to heat for 10–15 minutes until your fat or oil is very hot. When taking this out again, be very careful that your children are not running around in close proximity. I remember many angst cries of 'stand back' when my mother made it. But do make sure that the fat is hot enough, you may find that the Yorkshire pudding doesn't rise if it isn't.

4. Quickly pour the batter into the hot fat, place the sausages in the batter roughly spread out and bake for around 40 minutes or until the Yorkshire Pudding is well risen and golden brown.

NUTRITIONAL INFORMATION • Not much needs to be added to make this recipe a complete meal. It already has a good protein (sausage) and carbohydrate (Yorkshire pudding) source. Add a vegetable or two to make a perfectly balanced child's meal.

Thanks to Jane Cole, Mummy to Rachael and Jonathan for the Yorkshire pudding recipe and to Fiona Macfarlane, Mummy to Alastair and Oliver, for the idea for Toad in the Hole

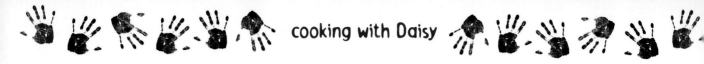

     cooking with Daisy

Cottage Pie

👨‍👩‍👧 Family food   ❄️ Freezes well   🍴 2 adults + 2–3 kids   ☺️ 8 months   🥣 30 mins prep   🔲 25 mins cooking

A great source of winter comfort food for children of all ages, not to mention their parents.

450g (1lb) minced beef
1 kg (2 lb 4 oz) potatoes
1 medium red onion
3 carrots
1 leek
1 medium pepper, red or green
6–8 mushrooms
400 g can chopped tomatoes
olive oil for cooking
1 vegetable stock cube
milk and butter for mashing
grated cheese for topping, optional
salt and pepper, if desired

A classic recipe that has all the ingredients for a complete meal: protein (beef), carbohydrate (potato) and vegetables (carrots, peppers, tomatoes). The beef is also a very good source of iron, essential for growth and development.

1. Set your oven to 200°C (fan 180°c), 400°F or Gas Mark 6. Peel and roughly chop the potatoes and put them on to boil for about 20 minutes.

2. While they are cooking, finely chop all of the other vegetables. Warm a little olive oil in a frying pan, stir in and add the onion, carrots, leek and pepper. Stir-fry for 5 minutes, then add the mushrooms and keep stirring for 2–3 minutes more. Remove the vegetables from the pan and place to one side.

3. Heat a little more oil in the frying pan and add the minced beef, moving it around with a wooden spoon to break up the lumps and to ensure that it browns evenly.

4. Once it reaches this stage, add the vegetables to the meat along with the tomatoes. Sprinkle the stock cube over the pan, stir and simmer for 5 minutes. While the mince is simmering, you can mash the potatoes, adding milk and butter to your own preferred consistency, and seasoning to taste.

5. Place the mince mixture in a suitable ovenproof dish and cover with the mashed potatoes. Grate some cheese over the top if you wish to give it a delicious crispy cheesy topping. Cook in the preheated oven for 25 minutes.

Once cooked, the cottage pie can be served as it is or puréed to your desired consistency.

Jemima French, Mummy to Meadow, Edie, Lilly and Dewi

Special Shepherd's Pie

👪 Family food ❄️ Freezes well 🍽️ 2 adults + 2–3 kids 😊 8 months 🥄 30 mins prep 🍳 30–40 mins cooking

You may be wondering why I've included a recipe for Shepherd's Pie alongside one for Cottage Pie. Although they are very similar dishes, the big difference is that Shepherd's Pie contains lamb and Cottage Pie contains beef. While many parents have clear views about not using one or the other these days, I felt it was important to include both.

450 g (1 lb) minced lamb
1 kg (2 lb 4 oz) potatoes
2 red onions, finely chopped
250 g (9 oz) button mushrooms, thinly sliced
2 tbsp fresh parsley, finely chopped
2 tbsp Worcestershire sauce
1 tbsp dried oregano, 1 tbsp dried thyme
400 g can chopped tomatoes
1 tbsp honey
2 tbsp plain flour
butter and milk for mashing
50 g (2 oz) grated Cheddar cheese
olive oil, for cooking
salt and pepper, if desired

NUTRITIONAL INFORMATION
Shepherd's pie is one of those classic, reliable, nutritious recipes. It combines lamb (a good source of protein) with vegetables and potatoes (a great source of carbohydrate). It's a complete meal in one dish.

1. Preheat the oven to 200°C (fan 180°C), 400°F or Gas Mark 6. Peel the potatoes and put them on to boil for around 20 minutes while you are preparing the mince.

2. Heat 1 tablespoon olive oil in a large frying pan or saucepan. Put in the chopped onion and cook for about five minutes, stirring constantly. Add the minced lamb and stir until it has browned nicely.

3. In another small frying pan, sauté the sliced mushrooms with the chopped parsley until all the liquid has evaporated.

4. Add the mushrooms, Worcestershire sauce and herbs to the mince and onion mixture. Bring it just to the boil and then pour in the tomatoes. Stir well to mix and add the honey (if you are going to purée this for infants under one, leave the honey out).

5. Sprinkle the flour over the mince and stir to blend, simmering for about five minutes. By now it should be a thick but not dry mixture. Season, if you wish, and turn into an ovenproof dish.

6. Now mash the potatoes until smooth with butter, milk and salt and pepper to taste if you wish, then spread over the mince mixture. Sprinkle the grated cheese on top.

7. Bake for 30–40 minutes and serve immediately.

Judy Starling, Granny to Jasper and Rohanna

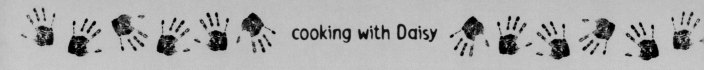

Mini Balls in Tomato Sauce

 Kid's food   Freezes well 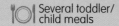 Several toddler/child meals   9 months   25-30 mins prep each set of balls  20 mins cooking

The friend who sent me this recipe tells me that it is inspired by Nigella Lawson who suggested making tiny little meatballs as a pasta sauce. Her 2-year-old, Jasper, loved the idea of eating the little balls so much that she began experimenting with the basic recipe to see what else could be disguised in this way.

This does take a little time to prepare but don't be put off since you can make lots of mini-balls in one go and then refrigerate or even freeze them, leaving you to pick-and-mix when you need a quick and easy meal. Because you will be freezing them uncooked, make sure that you don't use meat that has already been frozen and defrosted when making them.

For meatballs:

450 g (1 lb) minced lamb

1 egg

2 tbsp finely grated Parmesan cheese

1 clove garlic, crushed

1 tsp dried herbs (oregano, rosemary etc)

3 tbsp breadcrumbs

Simply mix all the ingredients together by hand and make into tiny little balls, about 2 cm (¾ inch) in diameter. Refrigerate to set.

For veggie balls:

vegetables of your choice, either single or a combination such as courgette and broccoli, for quantity see below

1 egg, beaten

2 tbsp grated cheese

1 tbsp finely chopped onion

1 tbsp dried herbs

2–5 tbsp breadcrumbs

Grate the vegetables in your food processor to make 2 handfuls and then mix with the rest of the ingredients by hand, adding the beaten egg gradually (you may not need all of it) until you have a firm dough ball. You then need to divide this up into lots of tiny little balls. If your mixture is too wet, add more breadcrumbs: if it's too dry, add more egg. Refrigerate to set or freeze straightaway.

For tomato sauce:

2 tbsp olive oil

1 onion, finely chopped

1 clove garlic, peeled and crushed

1 tsp dried oregano

2 x 400 g cans chopped tomatoes

2 tbsp tomato ketchup

200 ml (7 fl oz) boiling water

Heat the oil in a large saucepan, add the onion and garlic and cook over a low heat until soft and golden. Add the oregano, tomatoes, ketchup and boiling water and simmer for another 10 minutes, stirring occasionally, with the lid off. This makes plenty of sauce and, like the balls, can be frozen in suitable portion sizes once cooled so that it's ready to serve when you need it.

When it comes to putting it all together, take enough of the tomato sauce according to how many you are feeding, heat it in a pan and add whichever balls you wish to serve. DO NOT STIR until they are partly cooked, or they will fall apart. Simmer for 15–20 minutes, covering with a lid to prevent the sauce from reducing.

Alternatively, you can add the balls to tomato soup if you don't have a ready-made sauce to hand.

Bee Trim, Mummy to Jasper and Rohanna

NUTRITIONAL INFORMATION • Choose one or both of these balls and serve with pasta and potato for a perfect meal. The veggie balls are particularly good, as they include protein (cheese).

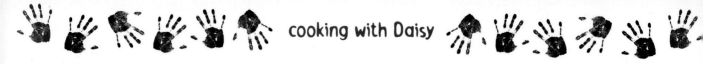   

Wilf had a Little Moroccan Lamb

Family food ❄ Freezes well 🍽 3–4 kids ☺ 6 months 🥄+🔲 35 mins total

Most children will eat any kind of meat when it's teamed with some of the sweeter vegetables. This is a savoury dish for the sweetest tooth, it has the delicious sweetness of butternut squash and the added bonus of the apricots.

It's good enough for adults too and I'd seriously suggest making enough for the whole family as it also purées perfectly for the youngest family members.

250 g (9 oz) lamb, chopped into small cubes
¼ medium butternut squash (deseeded)
1 medium onion
1 medium carrot
6 dried apricots
100 ml (3½ fl oz) home made vegetable stock (see page 82) or a suitable alternative such as
   Marigold Swiss Vegetable Bouillon Powder
olive oil for frying
salt and pepper if desired

1. Peel, deseed and dice the butternut squash and then set it aside. Finely chop the onion and gently stir-fry it with the cubes of lamb in a little olive oil so that the onion softens and the lamb browns nicely. Make sure that your lamb cubes are pretty small; if you go too large, you may find that it doesn't become tender enough for small teeth.

2. While it is cooking, chop the carrot and apricots into small cubes. When the lamb has browned, add all the vegetables and keep stirring over a gentle heat for 5 minutes.

3. Add the stock, season if you wish, and bring it briefly to the boil. Then reduce the heat and simmer for 15–20 minutes with the lid on, allowing the vegetables to soften.

4. Serve straight away (or purée to your child's desired consistency first) with rice or mashed potato.

Candice Raby, Mummy to Isabel, Wilf and Edward

NUTRITION INFORMATION
This is an excellent meal for the weaning infant, as well as for the developing child (and the whole family). The lamb and the dried apricots are excellent sources of iron and the carrots and butternut squash provide vitamin A, both of which are essential for normal growth and development.

Sausage and Bean Crisp

 Kid's food Do not freeze 3–4 kids 12 months  20 mins total

Just as popular with hung-over adults as with children! It must be those staple English Breakfast ingredients but they also make a delicious lunch or tea.

3–4 rashers of bacon
1 finely chopped onion
3 sausages (pre-cooked and sliced)
1 large can baked beans
1 packet plain crisps
grated cheese for the topping
olive oil for frying

1. Grill the bacon until crispy and then chop the rashers into little bits.

2. Fry the chopped onion in a small amount of oil, adding the slices of sausage, bacon bits and the can of baked beans once the onions have softened. When this is good and hot, pour it into an ovenproof dish.

NUTRITIONAL · INFORMATION
An energy-dense recipe with plenty of goodness. Baked beans, sausages and bacon are all excellent sources of iron and protein.

3. To create the crispy topping you need to hammer the crisps in their bag (make some air holes in it first so that you don't burst the bag) with a rolling pin and then pour the crispy crumbs over the top. Kids will love helping you with this bit. Grate the cheese on top and place under the grill for 5 minutes, until the cheese has all melted. Serve with a little mashed potato.

This is a recipe that you can change all the time. Leave out anything that your kids don't like or make a vegetarian version if you wish. For a really easy version, buy cans of baked beans with mini sausages and cut out some of the work.

Hazel Sellers, Mummy to Oliver, Harvey, and Rory

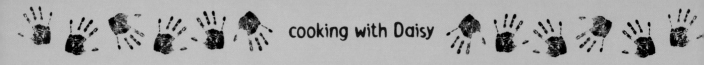

Kyle's Wiggly Worm Kebabs

 Family food Do not freeze 2 adults + 2 kids 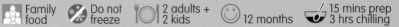 12 months 15 mins prep 3 hrs chilling 20 mins cooking

These are really a sort of glorified homemade sausage and testimony to the fact that children genuinely do adore flavoursome rather than bland foods. It's an incredibly simple and quick recipe and could just as easily be finished off on the barbecue as in the oven, but you do need to plan ahead in order to give yourself time to let the raw ingredients stand for a few hours.

3 slices of bread (brown or white)
500 g (1 lb 2 oz) minced beef
½ onion, grated (optional)
1 tsp crushed garlic
1 tsp ground ginger
1 tsp mixed cumin and coriander powder
1 tsp salt if desired
1 tsp chilli powder (optional)
1 egg
1 tbsp vegetable oil

1. Begin by cutting the crusts off and then soaking the slices of bread in water. Then, in a bowl, mix together all of the other ingredients.

2. Squeeze the water out of the bread and knead it into the mince mixture, creating one large meatball. At this stage you really need to let the mixture stand; cover the bowl in clingfilm and leave it in the fridge for about 3 hours or overnight if you can.

3. Once you are ready to cook the kebabs, heat the oven to 200°C (fan 180°C), 350°F or Gas Mark 4. Break small pieces of the mince mixture off and roll them by hand into thin sausages, about 1.5–1 cm (½ inch) thick. Place them on a greased baking tray and cook for about 18–20 minutes.

They are best served with warm pitta bread and plain yogurt (either as it comes or mixed with a bit of chopped fresh parsley and/or diced cucumber).

Farrah Pradhan, Mummy to Kyle

NUTRITIONAL INFORMATION

Don't be deterred by the spices, it is only the excessive use of salt in seasoning that should be avoided. In fact, spices should be encouraged as the introduction of more unusual flavours will help both to broaden your child's repertoire and encourage a willingness to try new foods.

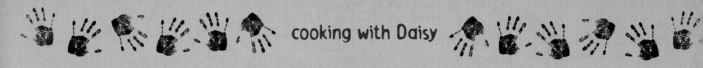

Corned Beef Hash

 Kid's food Do not freeze 4–6 kids 12 months + 50 mins total

This is really easy to make, stores well in the fridge and, served with ketchup or a little mango chutney, is really delicious. Don't be put off if you were served ghastly corned beef hash at school in the seventies and eighties – this is altogether different.

500 g (1 lb 2 oz) corned beef
1 large onion
700 g (1 lb 9 oz) potatoes
50 g (2 oz) butter
300 ml (½ pint) whole milk
salt and pepper, if desired

1. Chop the onion and peel and dice the potatoes into small cubes of about 1 cm (½ inch).

2. Melt the butter in a deep frying pan or heatproof casserole on the hob.

3. Add the onion and fry gently until soft, then add the potatoes. Stir the onions and potato together well and cook them over a moderate heat, stirring occasionally, for 5–10 minutes.

4. Next, pour in the milk, bring to the boil and season if you wish. Cover the pan and cook gently for roughly 20 minutes or until the diced potatoes are soft.

5. While this is cooking, dice the corned beef coarsely. Add it to the pan and cook for a further 15 minutes. It is then ready to serve as you wish.

A word of warning – don't stir too much or you will end up with corned beef mush. Just stir enough to mix in the meat.

Gill Cozens, Grandmother to Georgina, George and Edward

NUTRITION · INFORMATION

Corned beef hash is an excellent and affordable source of protein. This recipe is almost nutritionally complete, simply add one or two vegetables or follow with fruit for dessert.

Hedgehog

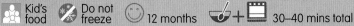

👪 Kid's food ❄️ Do not freeze 😊 12 months 🥄➕🔲 30–40 mins total

Good ideas don't have to be original ideas and, if you have a difficult eater, you'll know that appealing to their imagination is sometimes the only way to get them to eat. This is a sure-fire way to stir a little enthusiasm into even the most reluctant eaters.

Quantities should be dictated by common sense depending on how many children you are feeding but allow roughly 2-3 sausages and one medium potato per child.

chipolata sausages
potatoes for mashing
butter and milk or cream
Cheddar cheese (grated)

1. Grill or oven-bake the sausages until they are brown and cooked through. In the meantime, boil the potatoes and then mash them with butter and milk or cream to a fairly thick consistency so that you can make an oval mound of potato. This will be the hedgehog's body.

2. Poke the cooked sausages into the potato. Let your children help with this as long as the sausages aren't too hot. Finally, sprinkle with the grated cheese and place under the grill until the cheese melts.

Serve with plenty of ketchup and a vegetable. If you want to disguise your vegetable, mix some cooked frozen peas into the mashed potato before making the hedgehog's body.

Jeremy Mills, Daddy to Tom and Katy

NUTRITIONAL INFORMATION · If your child is slow gaining weight, add 1 teaspoon double cream per tablespoon mashed potato (increases calorie content), or 1 teaspoon cream cheese per tablespoon mashed potato (increases both protein and calorie content).

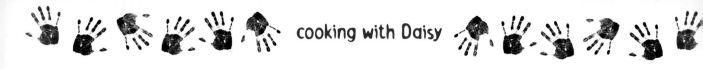

Tom's Tacos

 Family food   Freezes well   3–5 kids   18 months 🥄+🍳 30–40 mins total

Using tacos to disguise more healthy ingredients provides a simple, yet ingenious way of getting children to eat what they might usually reject. The mum who sent me this recipe told her 2-year-old that the tacos were crisps and they went down incredibly well from that point on. They are also fun to eat and children can add their own toppings such as grated cheese, finely chopped tomatoes or soured cream.

250 g (9 oz) minced beef
1 tbsp olive oil
1 small onion, chopped
2 tomatoes, cubed (skinned and deseeded, if you have time)
1 jar Uncle Ben's medium chilli sauce
1 packet Old El Paso taco shells

To garnish:
tomatoes (deseeded if you have time)
grated cheese
soured cream

1. Heat the oil and fry the onion and the beef together until the onion is soft and the beef has turned nicely brown.

2. Add the cubed tomatoes and cook for a further 2 minutes before adding the jar of chilli sauce. Uncle Ben's medium chilli sauce is very mild so you don't need to worry about it being too strong for small and less sophisticated palates.

3. Simmer the whole lot for 20–25 minutes to allow the beef to cook thoroughly. Towards the end of the cooking time, heat the taco shells as per the instructions on the packet. When they are ready, fill each taco with 1–2 spoonfuls of the chilli and garnish as you wish.

Store the minced beef mixture in the fridge or freezer, but be sure to make up the tacos at the last minute or they go soggy.

Clare Hall Taylor, Mummy to Anna, Tom and Marcus

NUTRITIONAL INFORMATION · Adding soured cream and cheese to this recipe makes it energy dense and a good protein source. Excellent for a child with poor weight gain or a problem eater.

4

one two three four five, once I caught a fish alive!

Fish dishes

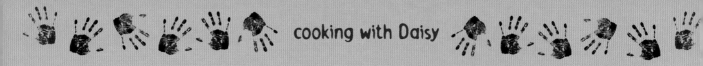

Fishy Dip Dip

 Family food   Do not freeze 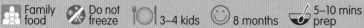3–4 kids   8 months 5–10 mins prep

Making a dip for children can be a great way to disguise foods that are otherwise commonly rejected. It also provides you with a good opportunity to give them a lazy TV dinner and either put your feet up for a minute or else get on with other things that you need to or would rather be doing.

Serve this with carrot sticks, peeled cucumber strips, small broccoli florets, breadsticks or strips of pitta bread. If you have a particularly reluctant eater and are at your wits end, try a packet of crisps, at least they'll be eating some of the dip with them.

This makes quite a lot of dip but it can be kept in the fridge for another day. If your child is anything like Daisy, split it into portions before they are allowed to dip. In my experience any leftover dip comes back looking pretty disgusting with all sorts of new soggy and interesting additions – not something that you'd probably want to preserve!

115 g (4 oz) smoked mackerel fillets
100 g (3½ oz) plain cottage cheese
100 g (3½ oz) crème fraîche
lemon juice to taste

1 Place the first three ingredients together in a large mixing bowl, having removed the skin from the mackerel fillets. Blend them all using a hand-held mixer and then add lemon juice to taste.

2 You can then create either one big pot of dip for children to share or decant into smaller bowls so that they all have their own private dip. Serve with the prepared vegetables and bread.

This is also delicious served as a filling for a baked potato. My son, Tom, who probably wouldn't count fish in his personal top ten, happily devoured it when I served it in this way.

Catherine Lapsley, Mummy to Callum, Jacob and Isaac

NUTRITIONAL INFORMATION
This is an ideal, and cunning method for promoting self-feeding for toddlers. This dip can be served as a complete meal combined with bread sticks or toast fingers and fresh vegetables and so is great for independent toddlers who believe they are fast growing out of being spoon-fed.

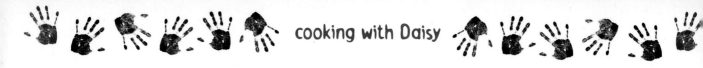

cooking with Daisy

Aunty Mary's Tuna Pie

Kid's food   Do not freeze   3–5 kids   12 months   20 mins prep   20–30 mins cooking

The best thing about Aunty Mary's Tuna Pie, from a mother's point of view, is that most of the ingredients come out of tins that you are likely to keep in your store cupboard, so it is something that you could probably always conjure up at the last minute.

potatoes for mashing
1 large can tuna
1 small can sweetcorn
1 can Campbell's condensed mushroom soup
butter and whole milk for mashing
grated cheese

1. Peel and chop the potatoes and then put them on to boil. Preheat the oven to 200°C (fan 180°C), 400°F or Gas Mark 6.

2. Drain the tuna and flake it into a shallow, greased ovenproof dish.

3. Cover with the drained sweetcorn and condensed soup and then, when the potatoes are ready, mash them with a little butter and milk and spread over the top.

4. Sprinkle with a little grated cheese and bake for 20–30 minutes until the top is golden brown.

Carole Bell, Granny to Holly, Kitty and Francesca

NUTRITIONAL INFORMATION
Ideally, children should have at least 2 servings of oily fish per week, and tuna is one of those. Oily fish provides the essential fatty acids children need for development. This recipe is almost a complete meal; add either a vegetable or follow with fruit for a wholesome meal.

Fish in Tomato and Parsley Sauce

 Family food   ❄ Freezes well   🍽 3–4 kids   ☺ 8 months   🥄 25-30 mins prep   🔲 15 mins cooking

This recipe was one of my grandmother's and a real staple of my mother's when I was growing up.

225 g (8 oz) cod or haddock, skinned and boned
3 tomatoes, skinned, deseeded and roughly chopped
25 g (1 oz) butter
25 g (1 oz) plain flour
300 ml (½ pint) whole milk
large handful finely chopped fresh parsley
½ small onion, grated
grated cheese to cover
salt and pepper if desired

1. Set the oven to 170°C (fan 150°C), 325°F or Gas Mark 3 and prepare the tomatoes.

2. Make sure that the fish is really well boned and poach it in the milk in a shallow pan on the hob for around 10 minutes.

3. Using the milk that you have just poached the fish in (and a little more if you need it), take another saucepan and make up a basic white sauce. Melt the butter in a small pan, remove from the heat, and stir in the flour until it is thoroughly combined with the butter into a paste. Return the pan to a medium heat and start to add the milk, very gradually, stirring constantly. You may find you don't need all of the milk, you may require a little more, depending on the thickness required, but it is very important to keep stirring to prevent lumps forming (a balloon whisk is best for this).

4. Cook the sauce gently for a further 5–10 minutes until the floury, starchy taste disappears and the sauce becomes tasty. Add the chopped parsley, stir and season if you wish. (If you are in a hurry or just want to make life easy, you can do this with ready-made parsley sauce.)

NUTRITIONAL INFORMATION This simple dish of fish in a tasty, colourful sauce combines a vegetable (tomato) with two protein sources (fish and cheese). The addition of carbohydrate in either mashed potato or rice completes the meal.

5. Add the chopped tomatoes and a little grated onion to the parsley sauce.

6. Place the fish (either whole or flaked for smaller children) in a greased ovenproof dish and cover it with the sauce. Sprinkle grated cheese generously over the top and bake for around 15 minutes until the grated cheese is golden brown.

Best served with mashed potato and peas.

Susan Smith, Granny to George, Daisy, Edward, Tom and Lottie

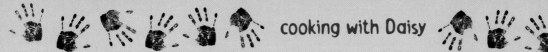 

Cornflake fish fingers

 Family food   Do not freeze   2–4 kids   8 months 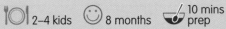 10 mins prep   10 mins cooking

This is a great way to make your own fish fingers with fresh fish rather than buying the frozen ones (although never a bad idea to have some frozen ones in store for those really 'last minute' meals). The 'batter' looks as orange as processed fish fingers so will be just as visually appealing.

1 egg
whole milk
2 handfuls cornflakes
6–8 fingers of firm white fish such as cod, haddock, sole
plain flour
butter and oil for frying

Firstly, beat the egg with a couple of teaspoons of milk and put to one side.

Now for the fun bit! Children will love helping to crush the cornflakes that constitute the crispiness in the 'batter'. Take a couple of handfuls of cornflakes and put them in a tough transparent bag. Use the bag from the cereal packet if you are near the end. Then hit it energetically with a rolling pin until you are left with crushed flakes but not dust (you may find that children won't want to stop so be careful).

Cut fingers of fish which should then be dipped firstly into the plain flour until coated, then into the egg mixture and finally into the crushed flakes. Make sure that they have a really good coating of these.

Shallow fry in a little butter and oil on a low heat for about 5 minutes on each side or until they are golden brown.

As long as they are adequately cooled they make great finger food and, if your child is anything like Daisy, should definitely be served with ketchup. Try serving vegetables with them that can also be eaten with fingers such as broccoli or cauliflower florets or carrot batons. You will then have a healthy and very self-sufficient meal for those who think they are far too grown up to be fed with a spoon.

Sonya Szpojnarowicz, Mummy to Max, Lukas, Jakob and Kaspar

NUTRITION INFORMATION

Perhaps the most well-known finger food, fish fingers are both nutritious and easy to make. Children should be encouraged from a young age to have fish at least twice a week, as it is not only a good source of protein but also a valuable source of essential fatty acids

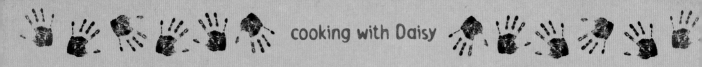

Romy's Tuna Burgers

Family food • Do not freeze • 3–4 kids • 12 months • 15-20 mins total

These are deliciously tasty but perhaps designed for the slightly more sophisticated palate. If your child is a good fish eater and willing to give things a try, I would definitely recommend them. If not, make them for yourself, you won't regret it.

Children will love helping you to make them since shaping the burgers requires bare hands and they can be as big or small as the hands making them. If children think they have made their own individual tuna burger, they may well feel more predisposed to actually eating it once cooked.

2 fresh tuna steaks
good handful of fresh mixed herbs such as basil, mint, parsley or coriander
1 heaped tbsp pickled ginger

optional sauce:
juice of 1 lime
2 dessertspoons soy sauce
1 chilli, deseeded and chopped
1 clove garlic, crushed

1. Mash up the raw tuna with a fork or masher in a bowl. Roughly chop the herbs and ginger. Mix all of the ingredients together in a bowl.

2. This is the messy bit. Using your hands and/or little helping hands, pat the mixture into fishcakes. You can either make lots of little ones or a few big ones.

3. These are best shallow fried in a small amount of olive oil. They will probably need a couple of minutes on each side depending on how thick you have made them. They also work very well on a barbecue, weather permitting.

If you are making this for older children or even adults, you may want to make this sauce to go with them. Take equal quantities of lime juice and soy sauce and mix with 1 deseeded, chopped chilli, a crushed garlic clove and a little water. Pour over the burgers.

Lady Cosima Somerset, Mummy to Romy

NUTRITION INFORMATION: Tuna is an excellent source of protein as well as essential fatty acids. Let children help shape these burgers with their hands; it will be messy but this sort of activity is so good for the development of manual skills and may encourage the reluctant eater to try something new.

Smoked Salmon Soufflé Omelette

🧑‍🍼 Family food   ❄️ Do not freeze   🍴 3–4 kids   ☺ 8 months   🥄+🔲 15 mins total

Don't be put off if you think this sounds too sophisticated for kids, it's actually a doddle to make. Take care not to overcook – the perfect omelette is one just tinged with gold on the surface but is still very soft and squidgy on the inside. Serve it with crusty bread for a luxurious breakfast, healthy children's tea or light supper for adults.

115 g (4 oz) smoked salmon, cut into small pieces (trimmings are fine)
2 tbsp double cream
4 large eggs, separated
15 g (½ oz) unsalted butter
2 tbsp snipped fresh chives
salt and freshly ground black pepper if desired

NUTRITION INFORMATION

Omelettes are a great, easy way to serve eggs to children. This recipe has the added advantage of including an oily fish (smoked salmon), which provides the child with essential fatty acids. Both a vegetable and carbohydrate such as toast soldiers need to be added to make a complete meal.

1. Place the smoked salmon in a small bowl and pour over the double cream, stirring to coat. Set aside for 10 minutes to allow the salmon to soak up the cream, stirring occasionally. This will make the salmon much more moist and prevent it from drying out while cooking.

2. Separate the eggs and place the yolks and whites into different bowls. Beat the yolks with a fork and season with salt and pepper if desired.

3. Place a 20 cm (8 inch) omelette pan or frying pan on a low heat to warm up and preheat the grill.

4. Whisk the egg whites with either an electric whisk or a balloon whisk until they form soft peaks. Add the butter to the pan and increase the heat, then quickly fold the egg yolks into the whites, along with the smoked salmon mixture and chives.

5. When the butter is foaming, pour in the egg mixture, shaking the pan so that it spreads evenly. Cook for 2 minutes, then loosen the edges with a palette knife and place under the grill, about 10 cm (4 inches) from the heat for another minute or so until lightly golden. Remove the pan from the heat and cover the pan with a warmed upside-down serving plate and then turn the two over together so that the omelette is now on the plate. Fold the omelette over to serve.

This recipe was kindly sent to me by the food writer, Orla Broderick

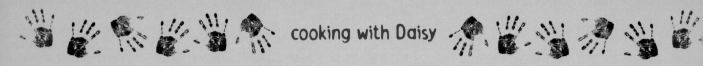

Griddled Salmon

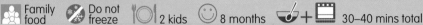

Family food · Do not freeze · 2 kids · 8 months · 30–40 mins total

This recipe was sent to me by a friend who says that her children enjoy almost anything cooked in a griddle pan. It is a great, healthy and quick way to cook food for children or adults but, if you don't have a griddle pan, this recipe can just as easily be grilled and is delicious cooked on the barbecue when the weather allows. This is an adaptation from Susannah Olivier's fantastic book *What should I feed my baby?*

1 skinned salmon fillet (or tuna steak)
1 tsp sesame oil
1 tbsp soy sauce
1 tsp balsamic vinegar
1 clove garlic (crushed)
selection of preferred vegetables (eg potatoes, sweet potatoes, courgette, carrots)

1. Start by marinating the fish in a small dish with the oil, soy sauce, vinegar, crushed garlic and 2 tablespoons water, for 15–30 minutes at least. Marinating might seem like an avoidable hassle when you've got children tearing around the house but it makes such a difference to the flavour and, almost more importantly with children, the texture. If you are defrosting the fish, you can put it straight in the marinade in a covered container in the fridge, then it's all ready to go when you need it.

2. When you are ready to cook, start by preparing your vegetables, cutting them into fairly thin strips and then lightly steaming them. Something that I recommend for every kitchen is a simple steamer. You can buy small ones that just sit over a normal saucepan or go the whole hog and get one of those multi-layered ones that are great. Either way, a really useful thing to have. Don't overdo the vegetables here since they are going to go in the griddle pan afterwards. They really just need softening slightly at this stage.

3. Then cut the salmon into strips, heat the griddle pan until very hot and place the strips of fish and vegetables onto it. Turn everything once so that you get the nice griddled lines on both sides.

Serve with your child's favourite must-have sauce.

Anya Beatty, Mummy to Matty and Daniel

NUTRITIONAL INFORMATION

Both salmon and tuna are oily fish that provide the growing child with essential fatty acids. These fish are excellent sources of protein which, when combined with potato and one or two vegetables as suggested, provide a complete and attractive meal. This is also excellent finger food for a toddler.

cooking with Daisy

Herby Salmon with Crème Fraîche

Family food • Do not freeze • 1–2 kids • 8 months • 10 mins total

This is a fabulously tasty recipe for all children (and their parents) but great for those who are constantly running around or in need of extra calories; it was sent to me by a great friend of mine whose son, Joe, was born with a severe heart condition. Cooking for him was always a challenge because he needed lots of extra calories to help his heart work as hard as it could. This was one of Joe's favourites.

1 salmon fillet, carefully boned and skinned
handful of finely chopped fresh herbs, such as dill, parsley and tarragon
knob of unsalted butter
1 tsp olive oil
½ small clove of garlic, crushed or finely chopped (optional)
2 dessertspoons full fat crème fraîche

1. Cut the salmon into roughly 2.5-cm (1-inch) cubed chunks and press into the chopped herbs.

2. Melt the butter together with the olive oil in a non-stick frying pan and add the garlic until it sizzles.

3. Add the salmon cubes and fry gently for 3–4 minutes, constantly moving them around the pan so that they cook through. Next, add the crème fraîche and stir gently until hot throughout.

4. When you are satisfied that the fish is thoroughly cooked, remove it from the frying pan and flake it gently into the sauce using 2 forks. This gives you another chance to check carefully for bones. Serve as it is or puréed further with peas and mashed potato or pasta.

Sally Gandon, Mummy to Joe, Rosie and Phoebe

NUTRITIONAL INFORMATION
Salmon is an oily fish that provides children with essential fatty acids needed for normal development. This recipe is ideal for the small or fussy eater as a small portion contains a high amount of protein and calories.

Kid's Kedgeree

 Kid's food | Do not freeze | 3–4 kids | 8 months | 25-30 mins total

This is a very child-friendly version of real kedgeree and pretty parent-friendly too since it uses a can of tuna so that you don't even have to cook the fish.

115 g (4 oz) long grain rice
200 g (7 oz) can tuna
55 g (2 oz) butter
170 g (6 oz) can evaporated milk
2 hard-boiled eggs, finely chopped
½ tsp paprika (or cayenne pepper)
1 tbsp chopped fresh parsley
salt and pepper if desired

This recipe is ideal for the difficult eater, as it contains a lot of goodness in a small portion. It contains protein sources in the egg as well as fish, both of which provide essential fatty acids. Serve with a vegetable or with a fruit dessert for a complete meal.

1. Cook the rice according to the instructions on the packet and drain and flake the tuna.

2. Melt the butter in a large frying pan, add the cooked rice and stir-fry gently for 2–3 minutes, coating all the grains in butter.

3. Stir in the evaporated milk and add the flaked fish, chopped eggs and paprika, keeping half of one yolk separate to garnish the kedgeree before serving.

4. Continue to stir over a gentle heat for around 5 minutes and season at this point if you wish.

5. Serve straight away, garnished with the chopped egg yolk and sprinkled with parsley.

Brenda Klafkowski, Babcia to Sarah, Daisy, Tom and Lottie

5

pasta, rice and all things nice!

Speaks for itself!

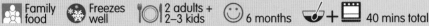

Finbar's Veggie Spag Bol

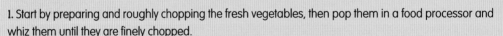

 Family food   Freezes well   2 adults + 2–3 kids   6 months   + 40 mins total

Mary Cadogan is Food Director of the BBC *Good Food Magazine* and has two grown-up children, Finbar and Austin. She very kindly sent me this recipe for vegetarian spag bol that was created by Finbar and is regularly cooked by the whole family. This freezes well, so if you have a freezer, make more than you need so that you've got a super-healthy meal for a day when you feel less inclined to cook.

For the sauce:

1 onion
1 carrot
1 stick of celery
1 red pepper, deseeded
2 tbsp olive oil
100 g (3½ oz) red lentils
400 g can tomatoes
600 ml (1 pint) homemade vegetable stock (see page 82 or
    use a suitable alternative such as Marigold Swiss
    Vegetable Bouillon Powder)
2 tsp dried oregano
½ tsp ground cinnamon

NUTRITIONAL INFORMATION • This recipe uses lentils, which are an excellent source of protein and a store cupboard essential. It also introduces new flavours: cinnamon, oregano and celery. This is a complete meal and ideal for the fussy eater who refuses to eat vegetables, which are so well disguised in this recipe.

To serve:

spaghetti or pasta of your choice
grated Parmesan cheese
salt and pepper

1. Start by preparing and roughly chopping the fresh vegetables, then pop them in a food processor and whiz them until they are finely chopped.

2. Heat the oil in a large saucepan and fry the chopped vegetables for about 8 minutes until they are soft.

3. Stir in the lentils, tomatoes, stock, oregano and cinnamon. Bring to the boil then reduce the heat, cover, and simmer for 20 minutes. Season, if desired, then simmer for a further 5 minutes.

The sauce is now ready to serve with your preferred pasta. For younger siblings, you can take some of the cooked pasta and sauce and whiz the whole lot again in the food processor until you have a veggie pasta purée.

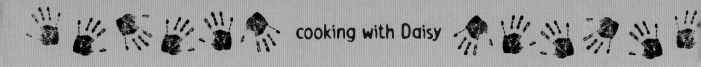

 cooking with Daisy

Mushroom Pasta

👪 Kid's food 🚫 Do not freeze 🍽 2–3 kids ☺ 6 months 🥄+🗓 15–20 mins total

This is a pasta sauce that can be puréed to your desired consistency and so can be given to babies from around 6 months with tiny baby pasta shapes or mixed with any grown-up pasta for older mouths.

6 spring onions
200 g (7 oz) button mushrooms
1 clove garlic, crushed
1 tbsp Philadelphia cheese
butter for frying
grated Parmesan cheese to serve if desired
your choice of pasta to serve

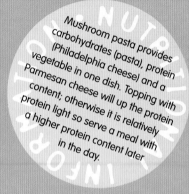

NUTRITIONAL INFORMATION

Mushroom pasta provides carbohydrates (pasta), protein (Philadelphia cheese) and a vegetable in one dish. Topping with Parmesan cheese will up the protein content; otherwise it is relatively protein light so serve a meal with a higher protein content later in the day.

1. Put your preferred pasta on to cook according to the instructions on the packet.

2. While this is cooking, finely chop the spring onions and mushrooms and then gently fry the spring onions with the crushed garlic in a little butter.

3. Once they have softened, add the mushrooms. Cook over a gentle heat for a further 5 minutes until the mushrooms have also softened. Add the Philadelphia cheese and stir until it has completely melted into the buttery sauce.

Serve immediately, either puréed or as it comes, mixed well with your chosen pasta and sprinkled liberally with Parmesan.

Sarah Kerr, Mummy to Isabel, Natasha and Imogen

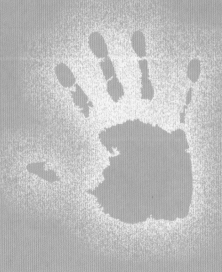

Creamy Chicken Risotto

 Family food Do not freeze 3–4 kids ☺ 8 months 🥄+ 🍲 20–25 mins total

I would seriously advise making double quantities here as it is as good for an adult supper as it is for a child's lunch or tea.

50 g (2 oz) butter
140 g (5 oz) Arborio or other risotto rice
1 large chicken breast, chopped
1 courgette, chopped
2 handfuls frozen peas
600 ml (1 pint) homemade stock (see page 82 or use a suitable alternative such as Marigold Swiss Vegetable Bouillon Powder)
1–2 tbsp Philadelphia cheese

1 Melt the butter in a saucepan and add the rice. Cook the rice on a gentle heat for about 5 minutes making sure that it all gets evenly coated with the butter.

2 Add the chopped chicken and continue to stir for a further 5 minutes so that the chicken browns slightly. Add the courgette and frozen peas and stir.

3 Now start to add the chicken stock. You need to do this a ladleful at a time, stirring constantly, only adding the next ladleful when the previous one is absorbed, until the rice expands and becomes fluffy. This will take around 15–20 minutes. Once you are happy with the consistency, remove the pan from the heat and stir in the Philadelphia for a really creamy risotto.

This works very well puréed for smaller mouths so you can feed the whole family in one fell swoop.

Elly Bailey, Mummy to Honor and Livia

NUTRITIONAL INFORMATION

Risotto is an easy and nutritious recipe that can be served as a complete meal. Disguise more vegetables in this for the reluctant vegetable eater or add more cream cheese for the difficult eater with a low weight gain.

Linguine with In-and-Out-of-the-Pan Tomato and Basil Sauce

 Family food   Do not freeze   2 adults + 2–4 kids 😊 8 months   10 mins total

This is a simple, summery pasta dish that tastes great. If you have the time or the inclination, it is best to remove the tomato skins first. Cover them with boiling water for 30 seconds, drain and refresh under cold water. The skins will now come away easily.

400–500 g (about 14–18 oz) dried linguine (or pasta of your choice)
5 tbsp extra virgin olive oil
2 shallots, peeled and finely chopped
8 large, well-flavoured tomatoes, deseeded and roughly chopped into small cubes
1 tsp caster sugar
large handful of fresh basil leaves, roughly torn
small handful of fresh parsley leaves, chopped
salt and pepper

1. Once you have chopped and prepared your ingredients, start cooking the linguine or your preferred pasta in plenty of boiling water according to the instructions on the packet before you begin to make the sauce.

2. Put 2 tablespoons of the olive oil into a large frying pan and place it over a low heat. When the oil is hot, tip in the shallots and fry them gently for a few minutes, until soft and slightly golden. Increase the heat to medium–high, add the tomatoes and sugar, and cook them for about 45 seconds, stirring. Add the basil and parsley, and season with a little salt and black pepper if desired. Cook for a further 30 seconds, still stirring, remove the pan from the heat.

3. Quickly drain the pasta, toss it in the remaining olive oil, and divide it between the bowls. Return the frying pan to the hob for just long enough to re-heat the sauce, if necessary, then pour it over the pasta, and serve immediately.

Ruth Watson, award-winning cookery writer and owner of the Crown and Castle Hotel in Suffolk

NUTRITION INFORMATION

Pasta is a great source of carbohydrate and children love the different shapes and sizes that go to make varied dishes. The fresh tomato sauce is an ideal and healthy accompaniment and is full of vitamin C. Add a protein source, such as grated Parmesan, to make a complete meal.

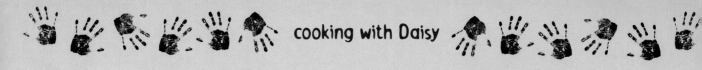

Cara's Fantastic Veggie Pasta Sauce

Kid's food | Freezes well | 4–5 kids | 6 months | 30 mins total

Children love pasta and this sauce gives you a fabulous way of disguising vegetables that they may not be as keen to eat. There is a huge selection of pasta for small mouths available at most supermarkets these days, even tiny shapes small enough for babies. However, if you have a baby that doesn't do lumps yet, just purée the pasta along with the sauce.

2 carrots
2 handfuls green vegetables (broccoli/spinach/green beans etc.)
1 small onion, chopped
1 clove garlic, crushed
400 g can chopped tomatoes
1 tbsp tomato purée
1 tsp mixed herbs
½ tsp Demerara sugar
salt and pepper and a dash of balsamic vinegar to taste if desired

1. Chop all of the green vegetables and the carrots then soften them either by steaming or boiling. Put the carrots on first for 3–5 minutes and then add the green vegetables for a further 3–5 minutes.

2. While they are cooking, soften the onion and chopped garlic in a saucepan or high-sided frying pan.

3. Drain the vegetables and add them to the onion and garlic along with the can of tomatoes, tomato purée, herbs and sugar. Bring the whole thing to the boil and then reduce the heat and simmer for about 5 minutes, ensuring that the vegetables are now nice and soft.

4. If you wish to season with a little salt and pepper, you should do so now. A dash of balsamic vinegar can really add flavour if you've got some.

The sauce is now ready to serve with your child's favourite pasta, either as it is or puréed to your desired consistency. It freezes well as a purée in ice cube trays.

Philippa Hawkins, Mummy to Cara

NUTRITIONAL INFORMATION
Pasta dishes are generally very successful with children. Combining pasta with a nutritious source of vegetables makes it an ideal meal for a child. This particular recipe is very high in vitamin C, so just add a protein source, such as grated cheese, to make it a complete and tasty meal.

Frances Edgerton's Garlic Spaghetti Cheese

👨‍👩‍👧 Family food ❄️ Do not freeze 🍴 2–3 kids 😊 8 months 🥣 15 mins prep 🍳 20–25 mins cooking

This recipe has been handed down through several generations and apparently originates from a mother who ran a pub in Brighton in 1860! Children will love this cheesy, buttery combination.

115 g (4 oz) spaghetti
30 g (1 oz) softened butter
1 clove garlic, crushed
85 g (3 oz) grated Cheddar cheese

Preheat the oven to 180°C (fan 160°C), 350°F or Gas Mark 4, then break your spaghetti up into bite-size lengths and cook it according to the instructions on the packet.

While the spaghetti is cooking, mash the crushed garlic into the softened butter to make garlic butter. Drain the pasta once it is cooked.

Take a heatproof serving dish (roughly 600 ml/1 pint capacity) and create alternate layers of pasta and grated cheese, adding little knobs of garlic butter onto each layer of cheese. Season each layer with salt and pepper if you wish. The final layer should be grated cheese, topped with the remaining garlic butter. Place in the oven for 20–25 minutes or until golden and crunchy on top.

If you wish to add extra vitamins and make this more healthy, you can add layers of fresh, finely chopped tomatoes (best if you skin and deseed them first) along with the pasta and cheese. Season as required.

NUTRITIONAL INFORMATION
Introduce children early to new flavours like garlic. Teamed with a cheesy pasta, most are bound to go for it. Add tomatoes or serve with another vegetable, or fruit for dessert, to make a complete meal.

Easy Cheesy Macaroni

👨‍👩‍👧 Family food ❄️ Do not freeze 🍴 2 adults + 2–4 kids 😊 8 months 🥣 15 mins prep 🍳 20–25 mins cooking

This is so easy to make and is a really luxurious macaroni cheese that is as good for adults as it is for children.

400 g (14 oz) macaroni
400 g (14 oz) carton mascarpone
1 tbsp wholegrain mustard
200 g (7 oz) grated Cheddar cheese
150 g (5½ oz) ball mozzarella, drained and cubed
salt and freshly ground black pepper if desired

Preheat the oven to 200°C (fan 180°C), 400°F or Gas Mark 6, and cook the pasta in a large pan of boiling water according to the instructions on the packet.

Drain the pasta and return it to the pan. Add the mascarpone, stirring so it coats the pasta then stir in the mustard, Cheddar, mozzarella and some salt and pepper if desired.

Transfer to a heatproof dish and bake for 25–30 minutes until golden brown and bubbling.

NUTRITIONAL INFORMATION
This easy-to-make, three-cheese dish contains both protein (cheese) and carbohydrate (macaroni). It is, therefore, an ideal recipe for a child with a poor appetite as it contains a lot of calories in a small portion.

Silvana Franco, food writer and Mummy to Fabio

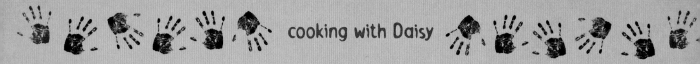

Sucky Spaghetti

Family food | Do not freeze | 2–3 kids | 8 months | 5 mins prep | 15 mins cooking

You may feel that serving spaghetti to children is a recipe for disaster and that all you'll end up with are messy kids and a messy kitchen. The truth is that you probably will. But while it can be chopped up for toddlers, making great finger food, it's a wonderful food for older children to experiment with. Learning to twist it onto their forks and shovel it into their mouths with the help of a spoon is a great exercise in co-ordination.

2 rashers lean bacon
½ a large or 1 small skinless chicken breast
handful of frozen peas
1 clove garlic, crushed
75 ml (2½ fl oz) single cream
75 g (2½ oz) spaghetti
olive oil for cooking
grated Parmesan cheese for serving

1. Start by chopping the bacon and chicken very finely. Heat a little olive oil in a pan, add the bacon, chicken and crushed garlic and gently fry together until the chicken and bacon are cooked through. This should take around 5–7 minutes.

2. Add the cream and simmer gently for a further 3–4 minutes.

3. Meanwhile, cook the spaghetti as per the instructions on the packet and throw in the handful of frozen peas for the last 5 minutes of cooking time.

4. Strain the spaghetti and peas and return them to the warm pan, stirring in the sauce.

Let your kids sprinkle grated Parmesan on top if they like it.

Zoe Brent, Mummy to Jordan and Leah

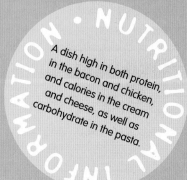

NUTRITIONAL INFORMATION • A dish high in both protein, in the bacon and chicken, and calories in the cream and cheese, as well as carbohydrate in the pasta.

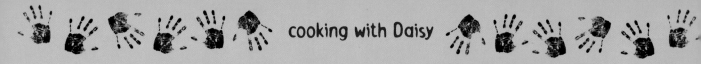   

Tuna and Vegetable Pasta Bake

Family food · Do not freeze · 3–4 kids · 8 months · 20–30 mins total

This is a simple pasta bake that can be made using fresh or previously cooked vegetables — great for using up any leftovers that have accumulated in the fridge.

185 g (6 oz) can of tuna, drained and flaked
selection of finely chopped vegetables (e.g. onion, courgette, peppers, celery, aubergine)
400 g can of tomatoes
200 g (7 oz) pasta of your choice
25 g (1 oz) grated Cheddar cheese
olive oil for cooking

NUTRITIONAL INFORMATION
This is a complete meal in one dish. It contains all the goodness a growing child needs – protein in the tuna and cheese, vitamin C in the tomatoes and carbohydrate in the pasta.

1. Firstly, you need to prepare your vegetable sauce. You can literally use any vegetables that you have and as many or as few as you think your child will eat. Chop them finely and gently fry until they have softened. If you are using a combination of leftovers and fresh vegetables, remember to add the pre-cooked vegetables towards the end just to warm them through.

2. Add the tomatoes, stir and simmer over a gentle heat for around 5 minutes.

3. While this is simmering, cook the pasta according to the instructions on the packet. Once the pasta is cooked drain it and put it into an ovenproof dish along with the flaked tuna. Mix them thoroughly.

4. Pour the vegetable sauce over the pasta and sprinkle the grated Cheddar on top. Pop it under the grill until the cheese has melted and turns a delicious golden brown. Serve immediately.

Justine Shenton, Mummy to Ben and Katie

Tuna and Broccoli Risotto

Kid's food Do not freeze 3–4 kids 6 months + 20–25 mins total

This is a recipe that uses a cheesy white sauce to combine the tuna, broccoli and rice.
It makes for a deliciously rich and creamy risotto.

100 g (3½ oz) long grain rice
100 g (3½ oz) broccoli, finely chopped
185 g (6 oz) can of tuna, flaked
25 g (1 oz) butter
25 g (1 oz) plain flour
300 ml (½ pint) whole milk
2–3 handfuls grated Cheddar cheese

1. Cook the rice according to the instructions on the pack.

2. Finely chop the broccoli and steam it over the rice for roughly the last 5 minutes of cooking time or until it is soft and breaks up easily.

3. While these cook, prepare your white sauce. Melt the butter in a small pan, remove from the heat, and stir in the flour until it is thoroughly combined with the butter into a paste. Return the pan to a medium heat and start to add the milk, very gradually, stirring constantly. You may find you don't need all of the milk, you may require a little more, depending on the thickness required, but it is very important to keep stirring to prevent lumps forming (a balloon whisk is best for this).

4. Cook the sauce gently for a further 5–10 minutes until the floury, starchy taste disappears and the sauce becomes tasty. Since this is to be a cheesy white sauce, you will need to add the cheese just as you think that the sauce is cooked and once the floury taste has disappeared. Continue to stir over a gentle heat as the cheese melts into the sauce.

5. Drain the can of tuna and flake the fish. Once the rice, broccoli and cheese sauce are ready, mix them together in a bowl with the flaked tuna and serve.

This is ideal for babies and can be puréed to make a finer risotto if you wish.

Sarah Gordon, Mummy to Madeleine and George

NUTRITIONAL INFORMATION · This recipe is not only nutritionally complete but also has the additional advantage of including a good source of essential fatty acids (tuna) as well as a vegetable rich in several vitamins and minerals (broccoli).

6

pease pudding hot, pease pudding cold

Ideas with vegetables

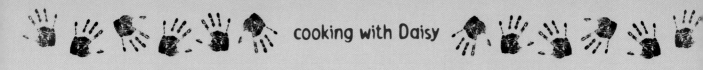

cooking with Daisy

Homemade Vegetable Stock

 Family food   Freezes well   varies   6 months   10 mins prep 1 hour cooking

Many of the recipes in this book list a basic stock amongst the ingredients. You can buy all sorts of stocks in supermarkets these days, ranging from cubes to powders to fresh stocks, and most of them are excellent. The problem is that, when you are cooking for the youngest members of your family, you need to know exactly what's going into their food and many of these stocks contain, for instance, fairly high levels of salt. It doesn't matter if your baby occasionally eats something that contains salt, but the general rule of thumb is to avoid using it until they are at least 12 months.

So the best thing to do is to make your own stock to ensure that you are cooking with ingredients that you are really happy for your baby to consume.

It sounds like a drag but it's incredibly easy and takes no time at all. Freeze it in batches and defrost what you need, when you need it. You can always dilute it with boiled water if you haven't defrosted enough and you will still get enough of the flavour from the stock.

To make a couple of pints of stock, you will need:

1 large onion
1–2 celery stalks
selection of 2–4 different root vegetables (such as carrot, parsnip, swede, turnip)
small handful of fresh herbs (such as parsley, rosemary, thyme; either mixed or just one of them if that's all you've got)
1–2 bay leaves
butter for cooking
about 1.2 litres (2 pints) water

1 Start by preparing all of the vegetables. For 2 pints of stock, I would aim to use at least one large carrot, one large parsnip and a medium-sized chunk of either swede or turnip. Peel and roughly chop them.

2 Heat a little butter in a large saucepan and sauté the onion for a few minutes until it has softened.

3 Add all of the other ingredients, bring to the boil and then simmer for about an hour with the lid on. (If you are making this with only older children or adults in mind, do season well at this point.)

4 Strain the stock, discard the vegetables and divide it into portions for immediate use or storage in the fridge or freezer.

Make chicken stock in the same way but use slightly fewer vegetables and simmer a chicken carcass in the water instead. If you've had chicken for lunch on Sunday, this is a wonderfully economical thing to do with your leftover carcass rather than just consigning it to the bin.

You may feel that making stock is rather worthy and a somewhat forty-something thing to do. Don't panic, you're not turning into your mother just yet and it doesn't mean that the local Women's Institute will be signing you up! It's just a great way to ensure that only the most appropriate ingredients make their way into your baby's and children's food.

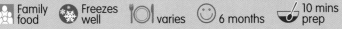

   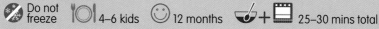 
Tofu Stir-fry

Family food | Do not freeze | 4–6 kids | 12 months | 25–30 mins total

This delicious and healthy stir-fry recipe was sent to me by Gary Lineker. His boys love this and don't feel too much like they are being coerced into eating healthy food because it tastes so great. For fun, try it with chopsticks.

2 tbsp soy sauce

1 tbsp chopped spring onion

2 tsp minced root ginger

150ml (¼ pint) homemade vegetable stock (see page 82, or use a suitable alternative such as Marigold Swiss Vegetable Bouillon Powder or a cube)

2 tbsp sesame oil

1 pack fresh tofu

2 tbsp olive oil

1 courgette, sliced

1 small bag beansprouts

6 baby corn on the cob, each cut into 3 pieces

8 baby asparagus spears, whole

8 button mushrooms, sliced

Combine the soy sauce, spring onion, ginger, stock and sesame oil in a bowl and place to one side for now.

Cut the tofu into roughly 5 cm (2 inch) strips that are about 1 cm (½ inch) thick and drain thoroughly.

Put the olive oil into a wok or high-sided frying pan and heat until smoking. Add the tofu to the olive oil and fry until golden brown. Remove from the wok and drain well on kitchen paper. Add all the vegetables (except the beansprouts) to the wok and stir-fry for 5 minutes. Then add the beansprouts, the cooked tofu strips and all remaining ingredients, bring to the boil and simmer for a further 2 minutes. Serve immediately with plain boiled rice.

If you like the sound of this but would rather give your children some meat, you could easily use chicken strips instead of tofu.

NUTRITION INFORMATION

This vegetarian recipe is a complete meal in one dish. The tofu is an excellent alternative protein source and the dish introduces new and interesting flavours such as ginger and sesame, as well as a wide variety of vegetables which could tempt the child who is wary of the 'unknown'.

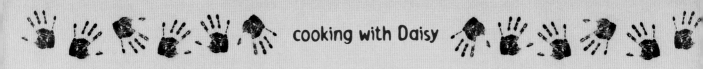
Eggs in Pots

 Kid's food Do not freeze 3 kids 8 months 5–10 mins prep 15–25 mins cooking

Baked eggs make a terrific meal for children. Not only can they help to make them but they can 'tailor-make' their own to suit their current whims or tastes. By simply adding ham, spinach, tomatoes or tomato ketchup, each child can have his or her own individual baked egg. Persuading children that they have chosen their own meal in this way can massively add to the appeal.

You need to bake the eggs in small, straight-sided ramekin dishes.

3 eggs (one per child)
30 g (1 oz) grated cheese
3 tbsp single cream
butter
salt and pepper, if desired

Tailor-made options:

Spinach surprise: 50 g (2 oz) cooked spinach.
Tomato surprise: 50 g (2 oz) chopped fresh/canned tomatoes or 4 tablespoons tomato ketchup.
Ham surprise: 1–2 slices of ham per person (wafer-thin sliced ham is the easiest to get into the ramekin).

1. Preheat the oven to 190°C (fan 170°C), 375°F or Gas Mark 5.

2. All of the ingredients create layers in the ramekin so let your child add his or her own layers. That way they'll know what they are uncovering when they eat it. Butter the ramekins and cover the bottom with one layer or a layered combination of the cooked spinach, tomato/tomato ketchup or ham. Add any salt and pepper at this stage if desired.

3. Carefully break an egg into each ramekin and then add one tablespoon of cream on top of each. Sprinkle with grated cheese and place a tiny knob of butter on top of the lot.

4. Stand the ramekins on a baking tray (remember whose is whose if they are different!) and bake them for 15–25 minutes, until the whites of the eggs are firm.

Be very careful to let the ramekins cool before serving (the contents will stay warm enough) and then serve with buttered toast or bread soldiers.

Sheila Harris, Grandmother to Rachel, Andrew and Matthew

NUTRITIONAL INFORMATION
Egg is a great protein source. With the addition of spinach or fresh/canned tomatoes and served with toast soldiers, this provides a complete meal. The addition of ham introduces a further protein source if you are not feeding vegetarians.

All-Round Ratatouille

 Family food   Do not freeze   2 adults + 3–4 kids   6 months    20 mins prep   20–30 mins cooking

I squirmed with smug, satisfied parental pride when Daisy learnt to say the word 'ratatouille' – or near about – at the age of around 16 months. It was a great favourite of hers. You can serve this up in many different guises and it is partly for that reason that I call it All-Round Ratatouille but also because it is great for all ages. You can purée it and feed it to toothless wonders as soon as they are eating combined vegetables or leave it as chunky as you like for those who prefer a little texture. For this reason and because it keeps well in the fridge (I've also frozen it puréed), I advocate fairly large quantities but feel free to scale down if you wish.

1 medium onion

1 clove garlic, crushed (optional)

2 medium peppers, either red, green or yellow

3–4 medium courgettes

2 small/1 medium aubergine

400 g can chopped tomatoes

Worcestershire sauce

olive oil for cooking

red wine or water

salt and pepper to taste

handful fresh basil leaves, if available

NUTRITIONAL INFORMATION: All the tasty, colourful vegetables in this recipe deliver a significant ration of vitamins (especially vitamin C) into a child's diet. If serving with rice, pasta or potatoes, add grated cheese to create a complete meal. Have a look at some of the recipe's serving suggestions for maximum temptation.

1. Finely chop the onion and soften it with the crushed garlic in a little olive oil in a large saucepan. Deseed and chop the peppers and add them to the pan.

2. Wash the courgettes and chop them into 1–2 cm (½–¾ inch) slices or cubes. Add them to the pan with the tomatoes. You may need to turn up the heat slightly here to get the tomatoes simmering, but as soon as they are, reduce the heat. Chop the aubergines and add them (purists would leave these pressed and covered in salt beforehand to drain some of the juices – do this if you have the time or the inclination but don't worry if not). At this stage you should season with Worcestershire sauce to taste and salt and pepper if desired. If I am making this for adults I would then add a generous slug of red wine; if you need more liquid for children you can still use the wine (it will just cook away, leaving the flavour), or add a little water if you prefer.

3. Cover and cook on low for around 25–30 minutes. You should stir every 5 minutes or so to ensure that all ingredients are well mixed and cooking evenly. Once it's cooked, taste it for seasoning and tear the basil leaves and stir into the pot.

Serve immediately or divide into portions for storing. Ratatouille is one of those tomato-based dishes that genuinely improve with time. I am happy to store it covered in the fridge with a lid on for up to a week and it will just keep on getting better.

Serving suggestions are numerous. Try it puréed with couscous for toothless wonders or with rice, pasta and baked potatoes for those who are a little older. Sprinkle grated cheese on top if you like (Parmesan or Cheddar) to add protein and flavour. We like to eat it piled high in a bowl, covered in grated cheese and with a great big hunk of warm crusty bread. It can equally be served as a vegetable and is delicious with sausages and mash, roast chicken or lamb

Marrow Mess

 Family food   Do not freeze   4–5 kids   6 months   25–35 mins total

Nobody ever really knows what to do with marrow – this is a great way of preparing it either as a dish in its own right or as a vegetable with whatever else you like.

30 g (1oz) butter
olive oil
1 medium onion, finely chopped
1 large marrow
4–5 tomatoes
1 dessertspoon plain flour
single cream
1 tbsp tomato ketchup
vinegar
salt and pepper to taste

1. Melt the butter and a tablespoon or so of olive oil together in a large saucepan. Add the finely chopped onion and allow to brown.

2. While the onion cooks, peel the marrow and cut it in half. You then need to deseed and rinse each half before chopping into roughly 1 cm (½ inch) cubes.

3. Skin the tomatoes by placing them in a heatproof bowl and cover with boiling water, leave for about 30 seconds and then rinse in cold water; the skins should come off very easily. Deseed them if you want to and cut the flesh into smaller pieces.

4. Add the marrow, tomatoes and a little salt and pepper (if desired) to the now softened onions. Stir well and simmer on a low heat with the lid on until the marrow is soft and translucent but not mushy. This may take up to 15–20 minutes, depending on the size of your marrow cubes. Next combine the flour with a little single cream in a cup and then pour over the vegetables. Mix well so that it combines with all the vegetable juices. Add the tomato ketchup and a splash of vinegar to taste and stir well. This is then ready to serve.

This can of course be puréed for your toothless wonders and so is great for children of all ages in whatever consistency they prefer.

Caryl Harwood-Matthews, Granny to Imogen and Harry

NUTRITIONAL INFORMATION

This recipe disguises two excellent vegetable sources – marrow and tomato. Create a complete meal by topping with grated cheese and serving with rice or pasta. You could even finely chop a chicken breast and cook it up with the onion to provide a non-vegetarian variation on this recipe.

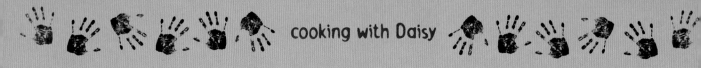

Cheese and Tomato Puff Tart

Family food | Do not freeze | 2 adults + 2–3 kids | 12 months | 10 mins prep | 20-25 mins cooking

This delicious tart provides gooey strings of cheese to play with or eat, whichever you prefer. I'm often put off by the mere sight of the word 'pastry' in a recipe but this is so easy and uses ready-made puff pastry anyway. Possibly one of the best inventions since sliced bread!

1 packet puff pastry
1 tbsp Dijon mustard
Emmental or Cheddar slices
3 medium tomatoes, sliced
1 tbsp olive oil
a few fresh basil leaves, chopped or whole
salt and pepper to taste

1. Preheat your oven to 180°C (fan 160°C), 350°F or Gas Mark 4, then roll out your pastry and use it to line a greased flan dish (roughly 20 cm/8 inches). Spread a thin layer of mustard on the pastry base.

2. Arrange the cheese slices on top of the mustard in one single layer and arrange the sliced tomatoes on top of the cheese in another single layer. Drizzle olive oil on top and add salt and pepper to taste.

3. Bake in the oven for 20–25 minutes or until your pastry starts to get slightly golden around the edges.

4. Serve warm with the fresh basil leaves sprinkled on top. (You may decide not to, it's amazing what the sight of 'green bits' can do to a child's appetite.)

Florence Sheppard, Mummy to Charles and Louis

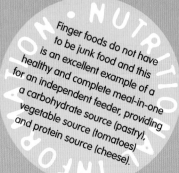
NUTRITIONAL INFORMATION • Finger foods do not have to be junk food and this is an excellent example of a healthy and complete meal-in-one for an independent feeder, providing a carbohydrate source (pastry), vegetable source (tomatoes) and protein source (cheese).

Filled Potatoes

 Family food
Do not freeze
1 medium potato per kid
12 months
5 mins prep
1 hour cooking

It's always a good idea to have one or two baking potatoes in your vegetable rack. They are so versatile and can be served as a meal in their own right with a few simple additions.

Everybody's made them with baked beans and cheese – a combination that actually makes a fabulously well-balanced meal – never feel that just because you are feeling lazy and unimaginative, you aren't necessarily giving your child a decent meal!

Here are some ideas for yummy variations

Firstly, bake the potatoes. They are at their best and crispiest if done from scratch in the oven at about 200°C (fan 180°C), 400°F or Gas Mark 6 for just over an hour, but if you've got hungry mouths to feed in half an hour, do them in the microwave, putting them in a preheated oven for the final 10 minutes to crisp them up.

If you are not in a hurry and can allow them enough cooling time, get your child to help you scoop the cooked insides into a bowl and put the skins to one side. Then mash the potato with a little butter and combine it with one of the following:

For a vegetarian meal:

All-Round Ratatouille (page 86)
Marrow Mess (page 87)
Tiny florets of steamed broccoli, soured cream and chopped chives

Or:

Tuna, sweetcorn and a large dollop of fromage frais
Fishy Dip Dip (page 54)
Granny's Bolognaise (page 37)

Finally, spoon the mixture back into the skins, top with a little grated cheese and pop them back in the oven or under the grill until it melts. Toothless wonders can also enjoy these (from around 8 months) but just give them the filling rather than the filled skins.

NUTRITIONAL INFORMATION
Potatoes are classed as a carbohydrate and not as a vegetable. Remember, therefore, that you will always have to combine them with a protein and vegetable to make a complete meal.

Carrot Fritters

 Family food Freezes well 4 kids 12 months + 30 mins total

Antony Worrall Thompson sent me this recipe for carrot fritters. They can either make a wonderful children's supper dish – they may not even know they are eating vegetables – or could be served as nibbles at a children's (or adult's) party. However you serve them, they make great finger food for independently-minded children.

They have the added advantage of being incredibly easy to make – don't be put off by the list of spices. You will need a frying pan and some very hot oil so be careful if children are around at this stage.

You can make the fritters whatever size you like, depending on how you intend serving them.

4 carrots
1 tsp ground cumin
1 clove garlic, crushed
1 tsp ground coriander
1 tsp ground turmeric
½ tsp Cayenne pepper
3 tbsp finely chopped spring onion
2 tbsp chopped fresh coriander
1 egg, beaten
150 ml (¼ pint) whole milk
140 g (5 oz) plain flour
sunflower oil for cooking

NUTRITIONAL INFORMATION

Carrots are a great source of vitamin A and this is a delicious way to serve them. Introduce spices into your children's food gradually from an early age to encourage adventurous eating.

1. Firstly grate the carrots (the quickest way to do this is in a food processor).

2. Combine the grated carrot with all of the remaining ingredients except for the oil. Mix well to combine everything together.

3. Heat the oil in a frying pan. When it is hot, carefully drop spoonfuls of the mixture into the pan and cook for 2 minutes on each side. Drain the fritters on kitchen paper.

Once cooled, they are ready to serve as you wish.

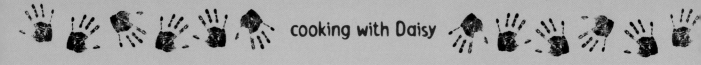

Sweet and Sticky Corn on the Cob

Family food | Do not freeze | 4–6 kids | 18 months | + | 15–20 mins total

Corn on the cob is fun to eat since it's a fairly messy finger food – this recipe ensures that it is also very sticky. These can be grilled or, better still, barbecued in the summer, at a safe distance and always under a watchful eye.

You can judge how much corn you will need depending on how many you are feeding and on whether or not it's the main constituent of the meal. The sticky sauce quantities can then be adjusted accordingly. Use the following as a guide:

4 corn cobs
2 tbsp maple syrup
100 g (3½ oz) butter
1 tbsp soy sauce

1. Chop the cobs into thirds or quarters depending on how big they are to begin with. Parboil them in boiling water for 4 minutes.

2. Meanwhile, melt all the other ingredients in a pan over a low heat. When this is done, roll the cobs in the mixture until covered. This can be done in the same pan but remember that the syrupy mixture will be hot so handle them with tongs or something similar.

3. They are now ready to barbeque or grill for a few minutes, turning them 2–3 times, until golden brown.

These are fabulous served with Honey and Mustard Chicken (see page 24).

Clare Hall-Taylor, Mummy to Anna, Tom and Marcus

NUTRITIONAL INFORMATION
Corn is a good source of carbohydrates and not a vegetable as many people assume. If serving corn alone for lunch or supper, complete the meal by adding a source of protein such as cheese and fruit for dessert. The raw kernels on the cobs should be sweet and juicy.

ED COLORS OF BENETT

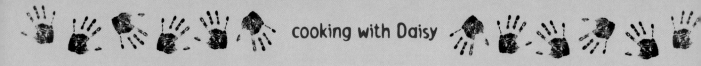

Veggie Soups

There's nothing quite like a bowl of homemade soup and, by making it yourself, you can be completely confident that all of the ingredients are things that you are happy for your children to eat. For instance, you'll know there's no added salt unless you include it. The other great thing about soup is that, by making a huge pan of thick soup, you can feed the entire family, from babies to grandparents if you wish. Here are three delicious vegetarian soups and a couple of cheesy serving suggestions to up the protein intake.

Thick Vegetable Soup

 Family food   Freezes well   4 adults + 3–4 kids   6 months   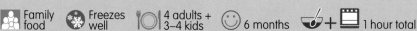 1 hour total

This is a cheap and cheerful recipe that enables you to use up almost any leftover vegetables (the following are only suggestions). It's suitable for the entire family, including babies who have made it to the combined vegetables stage and because it's so thick, it really feels like a good meal. The following quantities are generous but that's because it freezes so well that it's always worth making more than you need for another day.

4 carrots, 4 parsnips, 1 head of broccoli, 1 large leek
2 cloves garlic, peeled
1 large potato,
1 large onion
1 tbsp olive oil
30 g (1 oz) butter
850 ml–1.2 litres (1½–2 pints) homemade vegetable stock (see
   page 82 or use a good alternative)
dried sage
double cream/grated Cheddar cheese/chopped fresh parsley

> NUTRITIONAL INFORMATION
> Vegetables are easily disguised in this delicious soup and it can be tailored to your child's tastes and needs. Add cream to make it more calorie dense for a faddy eater with poor weight gain, or some finely chopped cooked chicken for a child who has a poor protein intake.

Prepare the vegetables: cut the root vegetables in 1–2 cm (½–¾ inch) cubes; divide the broccoli into florets; slice the leek and onion; chop the garlic. Heat the oil and butter together in a heavy-based pan and gently fry the onion until soft.

Add the remaining vegetables and the garlic to the pan stirring around until well mixed with the oil, butter and onions. Put the pan lid on, turn down the heat and sweat the vegetables for around 20 minutes, remembering to stir every few minutes.

When the vegetables are softened and a golden brown film has developed on the base of the pan, add the stock. It is important to scrape the brown film with a wooden spoon or spatula and stir thoroughly as this will impart a rich flavour and colour to the soup. Add a pinch of dried sage and then simmer, lid on, for a further 20 minutes.

Finally, blend the soup. A hand-held blender works well but watch for scalding splashes.

At this stage you can serve or divide up into portions for freezing. If serving immediately, dollop into bowls adding garnish to taste – a slug of double cream, grated Cheddar, chopped parsley and/or torn up bits of bread for dunking.

Angela Harrison, Mummy to Marlin and Matilda.

Frozen Pea Soup

👨‍👩‍👧 Family food ❄ Freezes well 🍴 2 adults + 2 kids ☺ 6 months 🥄+🎞 30–35 mins total

The best thing about this soup is that it uses frozen peas, which you nearly always have in your freezer. All the other ingredients are what I'd call store cupboard essentials, so it's a dish that could always be made at the last minute when you think the fridge is empty.

400 g (14 oz) frozen peas
1 small onion, finely chopped
1 small potato, chopped into small chunks
butter
1 clove garlic, crushed or chopped
600 ml (1 pint) homemade vegetable stock (see page 82 or use a good alternative such as
 Marigold Swiss Vegetable Bouillon Powder)
whole milk or cream (optional)

Melt a knob of butter in a pan and add the chopped onion, potato and garlic. Turn the heat right down and allow them all to sweat for 10 minutes.

Add the stock and peas then turn the heat right up again and bring to the boil. Simmer for 15 minutes.

Take off the heat and blend to a smooth consistency. You can now add some milk or cream if you wish to give the soup a more creamy consistency.

Sarah Kerr, Mummy to Isabel, Natasha and Imogen

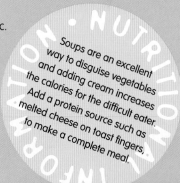

NUTRITIONAL INFORMATION • Soups are an excellent way to disguise vegetables and adding cream increases the calories for the difficult eater. Add a protein source such as melted cheese on toast fingers, to make a complete meal.

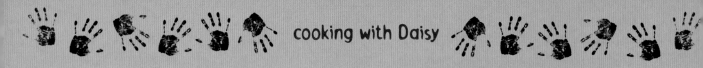

Daddy's Best Borscht

| Family food | ❄ Freezes well | 🍴 4 adults + 4 kids | 🙂 6 months | 🥄 20 mins prep | 🍳 40–50 mins cooking |

This was one of Daisy's absolute favourites and one of her Daddy's specialities. We discovered her taste for it one Christmas Eve when borscht is often served in Polish homes.

It's important to make a lot of this soup; everyone has seconds and it freezes well anyway so you may as well make lots in one go. For this reason, quantities are fairly generous.

5–6 medium raw beetroots, peeled and chopped into roughly 2.5 cm (1 inch) cubes
1 large onion, finely chopped
1 carrot, finely chopped
50 g (2 oz) butter
olive oil
2 litres (3½ pints) homemade vegetable stock (see page 82 or use a good alternative such as
   Marigold Swiss Vegetable Bouillon Powder)
juice of 3 lemons
salt and pepper to taste
crème fraîche and chives to garnish

NUTRITIONAL INFORMATION
Beetroot is an excellent source of vitamins (especially vitamin A and Folate). This recipe is ideal for children who refuse to eat vegetables, call it 'pink soup' and they won't know there's a vegetable in it.

1 Melt the butter with about 4–5 tablespoons olive oil in a large heavy-based saucepan and soften the onion in the butter/oil mixture for about 3 minutes or until transparent.

2 Add the carrot and beetroot, stir and sweat on a low heat for a further 10 minutes.

3 Add the hot stock and stir. Bring the whole lot to the boil, then leave it to simmer with the lid on for 40–50 minutes until the beetroots are soft and the whole thing is a great purple colour. At this point the entire house will smell fantastic.

4 Leave it to cool, then season with salt and pepper. It's best to season when the soup is cool enough to comfortably taste since the flavours will have settled by this time.

5 Blend into a thick purée with a hand blender. This can obviously get very messy in a sort of rather unpleasant *Reservoir Dogs* style if it splashes. If you keep the blender under the surface of the soup it will prevent too much splashing.

6 Add the lemon juice to taste, it should be pretty sharp but it's up to you. Re-heat when you are ready to serve.

Serve with a dollop of crème fraîche and chopped chives sprinkled on top.

A word of warning! Although, I'm sure that I don't need to alert anybody to the lethal staining properties of beetroot, only ever serve this to children in the kitchen in the knowledge that surrounding areas can be wiped down. The taste sensation outweighs the risks, I promise.

David Klafkowski, Daddy to Daisy, Tom and Lottie

To complete a soupy meal, serve with one of the following

Seriously Gooey Garlic Bread

This irresistible garlic bread comes from Sue Lawrence who has written many of her own cookbooks as well as being food writer for the newspaper, *Scotland on Sunday*.

I don't know many children who don't like garlic. Daisy adored it and was regularly fed garlicky lunches by her wonderful Polish nanny. This takes very little preparation and adults will love it as much as children.

125 g (4½ oz) unsalted butter, softened
3 large fresh or young garlic cloves, peeled, finely chopped
1 tsp coarse sea salt
150 g (5½ oz) fresh mozzarella, thinly sliced
1 'Ready to Bake' ciabatta loaf

1. Preheat the oven to 220°C (fan 200°C), 425°F or Gas Mark 7.

2. Beat the butter, garlic and sea-salt together.

3. Cut the loaf in two, lengthways. Spread the bottom half with the garlic butter and top with cheese. Clamp on the top half, wrap in foil, and bake for 20 minutes, until gooey.

Cut into thick slices and devour.

Grandma's Cheese on Toast

This is cheese on toast but with a tasty twist. The grandmother that sent me the recipe made it as a snack lunch for herself but her 2-year-old granddaughter immediately spurned her own cheese cubes and toast in preference for the grown-up version.

Quantities are irrelevant. Make enough for the mouths that you are feeding, using:

sliced bread
grated cheese (whichever cheese you prefer or a combination)
Dijon mustard
Worcestershire sauce

1. Toast the bread on one side and spread the other with a very thin layer of mustard. Sprinkle as much grated cheese as you like over this and splash on a little Worcestershire sauce.

2. Grill until brown and bubbling.

Sheila Passmore, Granny to Catherine

NUTRITIONAL INFORMATION

Either of these cheesy treats will make any of the vegetable soups a complete meal by the addition of both protein and carbohydrates. Alternatively, serve either as a light meal with carrot batons or with baby tomatoes and a little lettuce.

7

the dish ran away with the spoon

Favourite puddings

Lots of people write puddings off these days as calorie-filled indulgences, but they can play an important role in a child's diet, providing key nutrients and reminding your child that food is a pleasure, which is particularly important if you've had to work hard at getting the first course eaten. Try to introduce desserts that are both healthy and nutritious on a regular basis, but don't deny the odd indulgence. Just make sure that the word 'pudding' doesn't become synonymous with calorie-packed, nutrient-free treats. The following selection features what I'd call healthy, everyday desserts along with some wonderfully indulgent treats.

Here are a few hints you may find helpful:

• Introduce healthy desserts first as part of the weaning process. Fruit and yogurt should be served on a daily basis. This way, your child gets used to these first.

• Do not use desserts to bargain with your child to finish a first course. Instead, move from a tricky and unwanted first course, without too much ado, to a dessert that provides some of the nutrients that were previously refused.

• Try to add a nutritious element to every dessert, such as fruit. Remember that yogurt and milk based puddings provide a good source of protein.

• If your child is reluctant to eat vegetables, choose a dessert with lots of fruit and thereby ensure he/she receives all the necessary vitamins.

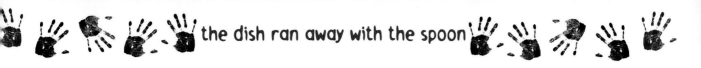

Apple Crunch

🧑‍🧑‍🧒 Family food ❄ Do not freeze 🍴 4 kids ☺ 8 months 🥄 15 mins prep 📟 30 mins cooking

This is basically a cheap and cheerful apple crumble. A very tempting way to eat fruit whether you are under ten, over thirty or anywhere in between!

175 g (6 oz) cooking apples
1 tbsp water, mixed with 1tbsp caster sugar
½ tsp ground cinnamon
115 g (4 oz) cornflakes, roughly crushed
55 g (2 oz) soft brown sugar
55 g (2 oz) butter, melted

1. Preheat the oven to 180°C (fan 160°C), 350°F or Gas Mark 4. Peel, core and thickly slice the apples. Arrange the slices in a deep buttered baking dish.

2. Pour the water, mixed with the caster sugar, over the apple and sprinkle with the cinnamon.

3. Roughly crush the cornflakes in a plastic bag with your rolling pin, tip into a bowl and, using a fork, mix in the soft brown sugar and melted butter. Pack this mixture evenly on top of the apple. Bake for 30 minutes or until the topping is golden brown.

Serve hot with yogurt, cream, custard or ice cream.

Sarah Herzog, Mummy to Anna

NUTRITIONAL INFORMATION
Disguising fruits in a hot pudding is an excellent way to get a difficult feeder to eat them. When served with cream or ice cream, this is an ideal dessert for the tricky eater or a child with poor growth.

Banana Ice Cream

🧑‍🧑‍🧒 Kid's food ❄ Freezes well 🍴 2–3 kids ☺ 6 months 🥄 5 mins prep

This is a delicious recipe, a great way to get rid of those old bananas and a cunning way to introduce fruit into a child's diet. It can be served to babies as young as 6 months and will probably continue to be a favourite well into adulthood.

You need to think ahead a little as the bananas must be frozen in advance.
2 over-ripe bananas
2 tbsp double cream

1. Peel the bananas and cut them into roughly 2.5 cm (1 inch) rings, place them in a plastic container and freeze them until they are frozen through.

2. Take the frozen banana pieces, place them in a blender with the cream and blend. Serve immediately.

NUTRITIONAL INFORMATION
Banana ice cream provides another clever disguise for fruit if you have a reluctant fruit eater. If you are concerned about your child's weight, you can serve the puréed, frozen bananas (let them thaw a bit) and omit the cream altogether.

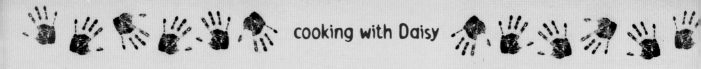
Smiley Oranges

 Kid's food Do not freeze 5–6 kids 8 months 15 mins prep

This takes very little preparation and is a great way of getting some vitamins into your little ones. You need to think ahead though, as the jelly-filled shells should be kept in the fridge overnight to set properly.

1 packet orange jelly
5–6 oranges (depending on their size)

1. Halve the oranges and squeeze out the juice very carefully, ensuring that you don't damage the peel or the shell of the orange. Scoop out and discard the rest of the pith from the skins and put the orange shells to one side.

2. Make up the orange jelly according to the instructions on the packet but use the fresh orange juice and top it up with water to the required quantity rather than just using all water. This will make the jelly wonderfully sweet and healthy. You want the jelly to be quite firm so use roughly 1½ tablespoons less liquid than the instructions suggest.

3. Using the orange shells as bowls, fill them with jelly, place them on a plate and put them in the fridge to set overnight.

When you are ready to serve, cut each half in half again and arrange them as you wish. They make a healthy and tempting pudding and great party food.

If you want to vary this recipe – and get more fruit inside your children – it's great with the addition of some pineapple chunks. Chop these up into small cubes and add them to the jelly before you put it into the orange shells.

Emma Milner, Mummy to Imogen, George and Harriet

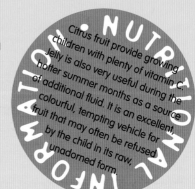
NUTRITIONAL INFORMATION • Citrus fruit provide growing children with plenty of vitamin C. Jelly is also very useful during the hotter summer months as a source of additional fluid. It is an excellent, colourful, tempting vehicle for fruit that may often be refused by the child in its raw, unadorned form

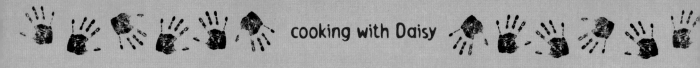

Strawberry and Passion Fruit Pavlova

Family food	Do not freeze	4 adults + 3–4 kids	12 months	15 mins prep	1½ hours cooking 15–20 mins to finish

This recipe was sent to me by Brian Turner, of the BBC's *Ready, Steady, Cook!* It is irresistible and would make a delicious pudding for a summer party or family lunch. I can guarantee there won't be much left. Remember that meringue is a great thing for children to make. They love to watch the egg whites turning into soft white peaks. Don't forget to let them help if you've got time.

5 egg whites
275 g (10 oz) caster sugar
seeds of one vanilla pod
1 tsp cornflour
1 tsp white wine vinegar
300 ml (½ pint) double cream
900 g (2 lb) strawberries
100 g (3½ oz) sugar
2–3 passion fruits
icing sugar to taste

NUTRITIONAL INFORMATION
Pavlova or individual meringue nests can be used to make many fruits more palatable for children. Remember that children eat with the eye.

1. First you need to make your meringue base. Start by preheating your oven to 160°C (fan 140°C), 325°F or Gas Mark 3. On a sheet of greaseproof paper, with a pencil draw a 30 cm (12 inch) circle (use a cake tin, plate or similar) then turn the greaseproof paper upside down onto the baking tray you will be using.

2. Whisk the egg whites until stiff, then slowly and gradually add the caster sugar then the cornflour, vinegar and vanilla seeds. Continue to whisk until thick and shiny.

3. Spread one-third of the meringue mix onto the circle you have drawn on the greaseproof paper. Use the remaining mix to build up the sides of the pavlova, finishing with peaks but making sure that they are not too high and fall over. Bake the pavlova nest for 1½ hours in the preheated oven. It should be crisp on the outside with a soft centre. Leave it to cool thoroughly and peel off the paper.

4. Whip the double cream with some icing sugar to taste, spoon this mix into the centre of the pavlova nest leaving some of the meringue peaks showing.

5. Chop one-third of the strawberries and purée them in a food processor with the 100 g (3½ oz) sugar. Cut the rest of the strawberries into quarters, mix them with the purée and pour over the pavlova and cream. Finally, scoop out the centres of the passion fruits and spread it over the strawberries, dust with icing sugar and serve.

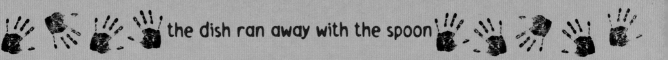

Cheats' Baked Alaska

Kid's food | Do not freeze | 5–6 kids | 12 months | 10 mins prep | 10–15 mins cooking

My mother made Baked Alaska when I was a child and I adored the fact that it was hot on the outside but frozen inside. I think that's where the appeal lies, kids will love this and it couldn't be simpler to make.

1 frozen Arctic Roll
4 egg whites
225 g (8 oz) caster sugar
salt

1. Preheat the oven to 230°C (fan 210°C), 450°F or Gas Mark 8.

2. Because it's so easy to make, I would really get the kids involved here. Firstly let them help to beat the egg whites, with a pinch of salt, into stiff white peaks. Whisk in 3 tablespoons of the sugar and continue to whisk until the mixture has gone soft and shiny. Fold in the remaining sugar.

3. Place the frozen Arctic Roll onto an ovenproof dish. Cover it with the meringue mixture ensuring that you leave no gaps, particularly between the dish and the meringue. It is important that the Arctic Roll is completely sealed.

4. Bake in the hot oven for 10–15 minutes until the meringue is golden brown. Serve immediately.

Anna Banfield, Mummy to Jessica, Chloe and William

NUTRITIONAL INFORMATION

This one is definitely a treat but is fun to make and incredibly easy. Ideal for serving to your children and their friends when they have been running around outside all day, burning off plenty of energy. You could up the vitamin C content by serving it with fresh fruit.

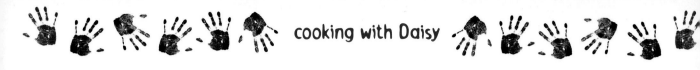

Microwave Meringues

 Family food 7–8 kids 12 months 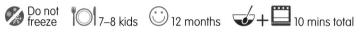10 mins total

These literally take minutes to make and the cooking time is seconds, so they are fantastic for impatient children looking for instant results for their culinary efforts. They will also probably be devoured in seconds, but do be careful since, as with all microwaved food, they will be extremely hot. My advice is to put them on a high shelf while they cool. The anticipation will be as exciting as the eating!

350 g (12 oz) icing sugar
1 medium size egg white
You will also need 2–3 sheets of greaseproof paper, cut roughly to the size of your microwave turntable. If the turntable comes out easily, you can draw round it. Make sure that you have some children's scissors in the house as, with safe scissors, this is the kind of thing they can get really involved in.

1. Sieve roughly three-quarters of the icing sugar into a bowl. Make a well and pour in a little of the egg white and start beating them together with a wooden spoon, gradually mixing in more and more egg white. When you have added all of the egg white, mix in the rest of the icing sugar gradually until you have a smooth paste. You may not need quite all of the icing sugar.

2. Using your hands, roll pieces of the paste into very smooth, walnut-sized balls. Place 6–8 well-spaced balls around the edge of the greaseproof paper (do not put any in the middle) and microwave on full power for roughly 45 seconds in a 900w microwave or 90 seconds in 750w oven. Please note that all microwaves cook at different speeds and you may have to try this once to get the cooking time right for your own oven.

Once they are cooked it is very important that they are allowed to cool. They can then be eaten immediately and are delicious as they are, with one side dipped in melted chocolate, or stuck together with whipped cream. For a healthy option, try some crème fraîche and a little fresh fruit such as strawberries or raspberries.

They can be stored almost indefinitely in an airtight tin. Make sure they are thoroughly cooled before storing

Diana Carter, Granny to Ben and Beth

NUTRITIONAL INFORMATION

Meringues are delicious when combined with crème fraîche and fresh fruit, such as strawberries and raspberries. The addition makes it ideal for most children who normally refuse to eat fruit. Not many would refuse a fruit-filled meringue basket or 'hunt the strawberry' among crushed up meringue!

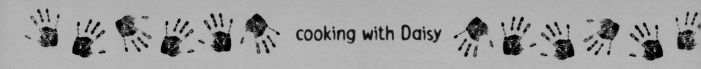

No-Bake Banana Cheesecake

👨‍👩‍👧 Family food 🚫 Do not freeze 🍴 4 adults + 4 kids 😊 8 months 🥄 20 mins prep 1 hour chilling

This delicious cheesecake has the advantage of a healthy ingredient – the bananas – so you can safely convince yourself that there's more to it than pure indulgence.

100 g (3½ oz) digestive biscuits
50 g (2 oz) butter
75 g (2½ oz) plain Philadelphia cream cheese
1 tbsp lemon juice
150 ml (¼ pint) double cream
25g (1 oz) caster sugar
3 or 4 firm bananas

You will also need a 20 cm (8 inch) loose-base flan dish or cake tin.

1. Crush the biscuits in a plastic bag with a rolling pin. Melt the butter and mix together with the crushed biscuits. Press the mixture into the flan dish to form the cheesecake base and put it into the fridge while you prepare the filling.

2. Beat the cream cheese and lemon juice together in a bowl. Add the double cream and beat until smooth. Next add the sugar and beat until combined.

3. Slice the bananas and fold them gently into the mixture. You want these slices to remain intact so don't overdo the folding.

4. Pour the mixture onto the base and chill for an hour or two. Remember if you are going to decorate this with more banana slices, do so at the last minute or they will go brown.

Sue Macartney, Mummy to Fiona, Alistair and James

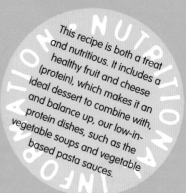

NUTRITIONAL INFORMATION
This recipe is both a treat and nutritious. It includes a healthy fruit and cheese (protein), which makes it an ideal dessert to combine with, and balance up, our low-in-protein dishes, such as the vegetable soups and vegetable based pasta sauces.

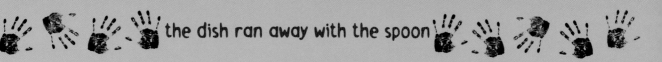

Crunchie Cream

 Family food   Do not freeze   2 adults + 2–3 kids   🙂 12 months   🥣 10 mins prep

This has got to be the ultimate in easy-to-create indulgence. You don't need me to tell you that this one should probably be served on special occasions or as a treat rather than every day. The best thing about it is that kids can almost prepare it themselves so long as you're standing in the background ready to leap in just in case.

300 ml (½ pint) double or whipping cream
4–5 large Crunchie bars

1. Whip the cream.

2. Crush the Crunchies in their packets with a rolling pin. Open the packets, pour the broken contents into the cream, fold in well.

3. Transfer to individual serving bowls such as ramekins and chill for 10–15 minutes before serving.

This can also be frozen and served as ice cream. You will achieve best results by freezing it, removing it when frozen and then blending the whole lot before freezing it again. Serve it with caramel sauce or, as a variation, try adding chopped fresh strawberries.

Ann Davies, Granny to Sam, William, Alice, Charlotte and Juliette

NUTRITIONAL INFORMATION
Definitely an indulgence that should be considered a treat but great fun to make. This recipe works well for the child with poor growth. Increase the vitamin C content by serving with strawberries.

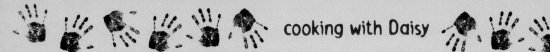
Ice Cream Sundaes

 Kid's food Do not freeze 3–4 kids 8 months 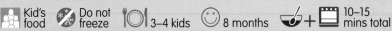 10–15 mins total

These were such a huge treat when I was a child and they take so little preparation. Kids will hardly notice that there is fruit hidden among the ice cream and sauce.

Vanilla, chocolate and strawberry (or any other) ice creams
150 g (5½ oz) raspberries, preferably fresh but frozen will do
80 g (3 oz) caster sugar
100 g (3½ oz) plain chocolate
3 tbsp water

To decorate:

chocolate chips
hundreds and thousands
wafer biscuits
crumbled cookies
dolly mixtures etc.

1. Firstly you need to make the raspberry sauce so start by rinsing the raspberries in a sieve. Then set the sieve over a bowl and push the raspberries through using a wooden spoon. You will end up with a bowl full of delicious raspberry pulp.

2. Add the caster sugar to the pulp a little at a time then stir the sauce vigorously until all the sugar has dissolved.

3. Next you need to make the chocolate sauce. Break up the chocolate and put it into a small bowl with 3 tablespoons of water. Suspend the bowl in a pan of barely simmering water, not letting the bowl touch the water, and stir the chocolate gently until it is smooth.

4. Then simply take your preferred flavours of ice cream and create individual portions using both chocolate and raspberry sauces. Let the children decorate their own according to taste and imagination.

Carolyn Gentle, Mummy to Peter, Michael, Edmund and Benjamin

NUTRITIONAL INFORMATION
Although ice cream is high in sugar, it still remains a good source of calcium, particularly for the child that refuses other milk products. It is also a good vehicle for fruit in order to tempt the child who is normally reluctant to eat it.

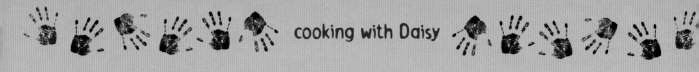   
Chocolate Fudge Pudding

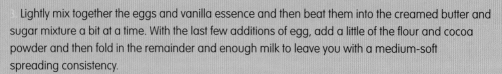

Family food | Do not freeze | 2 adults + 3–4 kids | 12 months | 30-35 mins prep | 40 mins cooking

This is one of those yummy chocolate puddings with a sauce that bakes underneath. It is fantastic served with cream or ice cream and provides great comfort food on chilly winter days.

For the pudding:

85 g (3 oz) self-raising flour
2 level tbsp cocoa powder
115 g (4 oz) softened butter
115 g (4 oz) caster sugar
2 eggs
½ tsp vanilla essence
1–2 tbsp milk
salt

For the sauce:

115 g (4 oz) soft brown sugar
2 level tbsp cocoa powder
300 ml (½ pint) hot water

NUTRITIONAL INFORMATION · This is a really delicious dessert and makes an ideal treat for all the family on those cold winter days when everyone has been burning plenty of calories playing outside.

Set your oven at 190°C (fan 170°C), 375°F or Gas Mark 5 then sift together the flour, cocoa powder and a pinch of salt and set aside.

In another bowl, mix the butter and sugar into a soft cream.

Lightly mix together the eggs and vanilla essence and then beat them into the creamed butter and sugar mixture a bit at a time. With the last few additions of egg, add a little of the flour and cocoa powder and then fold in the remainder and enough milk to leave you with a medium-soft spreading consistency.

Spoon the mixture into a well-buttered pie dish (roughly 1.2–1.5 litre/2–2½ pint capacity) and spread it evenly. Set this aside while preparing the sauce.

In a mixing basin, combine the soft brown sugar and the cocoa powder. Stir in the hot water and mix well before pouring over the top of the pudding mixture.

This should now go straight into the oven for 40 minutes. As it bakes, the pudding will rise to the top, leaving the delicious chocolate sauce underneath. Serve warm.

Sarah Stephenson, Mummy to Imogen and Olivia

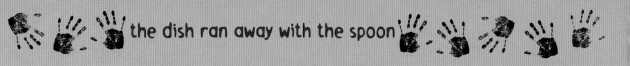

Pear and Blackberry Cobbler

Family food · Do not freeze · 2 adults + 3–4 kids · 12 months · 30 mins prep · 25 mins cooking

Another great way to disguise fruit, this time underneath these delicious, tempting cobbles.

5 pears, peeled and diced
450 g (1 lb) blackberries
250 g (9 oz) golden caster sugar
1 tsp ground cinnamon
knob of butter

For the cobbles:

250 g (9 oz) plain flour
4 tsp golden caster sugar
1 tsp bicarbonate of soda
2 tsp baking powder
1 tsp salt
50 g (2 oz) butter, melted
240 ml (9 fl oz) buttermilk

1. Preheat the oven to 200°C (fan 180°C), 400°F or Gas Mark 6.

2. Toss together the pears, blackberries, sugar and cinnamon. Butter an ovenproof dish and spoon in the fruit mixture.

3. Stir together the plain flour, sugar, bicarbonate of soda, baking powder and salt and set aside for a moment.

4. Stir together the melted butter and buttermilk then mix into the dry ingredients to make a sticky dough.

5. Drop spoonfuls of the dough onto the fruit then bake for 25 minutes until the crust is golden and the fruit is tender. Serve warm with a scoop of vanilla ice cream.

Silvana Franco, food writer and Mummy to Fabio

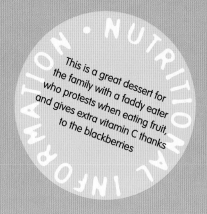
NUTRITIONAL INFORMATION · This is a great dessert for the family with a faddy eater who protests when eating fruit, and gives extra vitamin C thanks to the blackberries

Malt Loaf Pudding with Cinnamon and Orange

 Family food   Do not freeze   4 adults + 3–4 kids   8 months   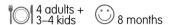 15–20 mins prep   40 mins cooking

This recipe was kindly sent to me by Nigel Slater. It is his twist on a classic bread and butter pudding and is utterly delicious.

10 thick slices of malt loaf or other soft fruit bread such as Sorreen
50 g (2 oz) butter for spreading
4 eggs
grated zest and juice of 1 orange
300 ml (½ pint) whipping cream
400 ml (14 fl oz) full cream milk
50 g (2 oz) light or dark muscovado sugar
ground cinnamon
Demerara sugar for sprinkling on top

You will need a medium-sized ovenproof baking dish (rectangular or oval) and a roasting tin that you can put the baking dish inside

1. Set your oven to 160°C (fan 140°C), 325°F, Gas Mark 3.

2. Butter the insides of the baking dish and then butter each slice of bread. Lay the bread in the baking dish so that each piece is slightly overlapping.

3. Beat the eggs lightly and mix in the orange zest and juice, the cream and milk and the muscovado sugar. Pour this custard over the bread. You may find the bread floats on top, but that's fine. Sprinkle a little cinnamon and Demerara sugar over the surface.

4. Half-fill the roasting tin with boiling water from the kettle and place it carefully on the oven shelf. Gently place the baking dish in the roasting tin. (You may find it easier to add the water once the tin is in the oven by pulling the shelf out a little.)

5. Bake for around 40 minutes until it is puffed up and very lightly set. It should still wobble when you shake it. Allow it to calm down a little before serving with double cream or crème fraîche.

NUTRITIONAL INFORMATION
This is a really delicious dessert that is high in protein. It is perfect to follow a protein-light first course. The orange juice will provide useful vitamin C.

Banana Custard

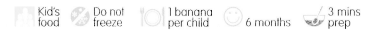

Kid's food · Do not freeze · 1 banana per child · 6 months · 3 mins prep

Both my grandmother and my mother suggested that banana custard be included in this book and, since I adored it as a child and Daisy couldn't get enough of it, I feel that four generations of women can't be wrong. Children love it and it's such an easy way to make them eat fruit without any kind of fuss.

It doesn't even require a list of ingredients as it's so simple. Slice a banana into a small bowl. Top it with a teaspoon or two of strawberry or raspberry jam and pour custard over the top. Et voilà!

When I made this for Daisy I used to buy those small cartons of ready-to-eat Ambrosia custard which means you can make this in about 30 seconds flat. I also used to leave the jam out sometimes for a less sugary option and it still went down very well. I doubt very much that anybody will want to make this any more arduous than that, but feel free to make your own custard if you wish to be more of a domestic goddess.

My mother also suggests that you can make it with grated apple or pear for small children or slices for older children. You can also let them top it with polka dots, sugar sprinkles or whatever you might have in the baking cupboard.

This also reminds me of another trick that my mother used to pull to get us to eat fruit. She'd serve sliced bananas and let us arrange a chocolate drop on the top of each slice before eating. The goodness in the bananas definitely outweighs the detrimental effects of the tiny chocolate bribe and it worked every time.

Disguising fruit in this way is an easy way to complete a meal for those difficult feeders who continually try to resist fruit. It can be enticingly decorated and served in a variety of containers.

8

pat-a-cake, pat-a-cake

Cooking with children

Savouries, cakes, buns and muffins, biscuits and cookies, treats and edible presents

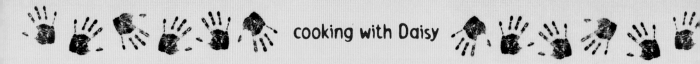

Daisy always liked to be part of the action in the kitchen. As soon as she was mobile she made a beeline for the dishwasher and would insist on helping me stack or unload. If I was busy and wanted her to entertain herself, all I had to do was give her a couple of pans and a wooden spoon and she would play contentedly for hours.

As she got slightly older, she progressed to standing on a chair so that she could see what was going on at work-surface level. Sometimes, to keep her amused, I would simply fill the sink with warm soapy water and throw a few of her plastic plates in so that she could 'wash up'. She loved to feel that she was engaging in 'grown up' activities.

When she became slightly more dextrous, we would bake together. I'll admit to several failures but also to some joint successes of which we were both fairly proud. But it wasn't the results that were important, it was the precious moments we shared while creating. These are the moments that are stamped indelibly in my memory and were the inspiration for this book.

Not only are times shared like this fun, they are also incredibly important in your child's development. Children will naturally want to explore objects and textures with their hands and mouths and should not be discouraged from doing so. In fact, those that are discouraged from engaging in messy play are far more likely to develop faddy eating behaviours and experience difficulties with the transition to more challenging food textures during the weaning process.

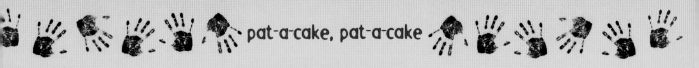

While, as adults, we are almost programmed to avoid messy situations, we need to let children get stuck in. Let them get their hands and faces covered in chocolate and let them eat half of the ingredients before they make it to the oven. Messy play is fun for children and it is an incredibly important stepping stone in the development of feeding and life skills. I have deliberately not suggested how much time each recipe might take to prepare in this section – don't rush, let them take their time.

It's not just young children that can benefit; cooking provides immense opportunities for exploration and learning for all ages. Weighing ingredients is maths, if you think about it. Spooning flour from bowl to bowl is great for a child's co-ordination. And all of our life skills are really learnt 'on the job', so start them as early as you like.

You may think that sweet and savoury treats are not the sort of things you want to encourage your children to eat. You're right, foods like these should be viewed as treats, but whatever you try to do to prevent it, your kids will crave and pester for treats at some stage. Encouraging children to make their own treats at least introduces an understanding of what goes into them and creates a sense of occasion around eating them. It's got to be healthier than an inevitable visit to the sweet shop. However, you won't find any nutritional notes here – there didn't seem much point!

Life's too short to avoid every indulgence so get stuck in.

Thanks to Diana Sarunic, paediatric occupational therapist, and Sandra Grosso, paediatric speech and language therapist, St. Mary's Hospital, London for their input.

Make-It-Yourself Pizza

Kid's food ☺ 18 months 🎦 5 mins grilling

These are a win-win situation for parents and children: for parents because the children do all the work, for children because they're great fun to make and fantastic to eat. A friend of mine told me that she did them for a children's party and not only were the children well-fed but they were also happily entertained for half an hour. The ingredients are not worth quantifying since it all boils down to common sense really depending on how many children you are feeding.

English muffins (for the pizza bases)
1 jar tomato pizza topping sauce
grated Cheddar cheese
mozzarella (diced or sliced)
slices of ham (wafer thin ham is ideal)

These are bare essentials but you could also add any of the following:
salami
sliced frankfurter
sweetcorn
sliced mushrooms
sliced cherry tomatoes... and so on

1. Slice the muffins in half, lightly toast them and give each child one or two halves on a plate. Encourage them to spread them with the tomato topping sauce first but after that, it's really up to them.

2. While they are creating, switch the grill on and once the pizzas are ready to cook, place them all on a baking tray (it's extremely important to remember whose is whose!) and grill them until the cheese melts. Serve.

If you don't have English muffins, you can do these on toast or on a halved piece of baguette for hungrier children.

Lisa Hynes, Mummy to Milo, Louis & Lara

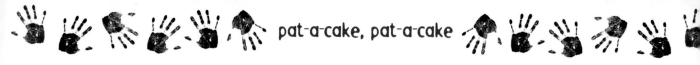

Savoury Curried Biscuits

 Family food   😊 8 months   📷 10–15 mins baking

These are amazing cheesy biscuits with a mildly spicy flavour that are as good served as a canapé for adults as they are a snack for children.

115 g (4 oz) butter, diced and softened
115 g (4 oz) plain flour
115 g (4 oz) grated Cheddar cheese (or use half Cheddar, half Parmesan if you prefer)
1 tsp salt
½ tsp mild curry powder

1. Let your children weigh out the butter, flour and cheese with a little help if they need it. Then sift the flour and salt into a mixing bowl.

2. Stir in the curry powder and grated cheese. Rub in the softened butter with your fingertips until the mixture comes together to form a soft dough.

3. Chill the dough in the fridge for 30 minutes wrapped in clingfilm. While it is chilling, preheat the oven to 180°C (fan 160°C), 350°F or Gas Mark 4 and grease a couple of baking trays.

4. On a lightly floured surface, roll out the dough into a fairly thin rectangle. Using a 5 cm (2 inch) – or near enough – biscuit cutter, cut the biscuits out and arrange them on the baking tray.

5. Bake them in the oven for 10–15 minutes until they turn a deep golden brown. Let them cool for five minutes on the baking tray and then transfer them to a wire rack where they should be left to cool and crisp completely before eating.

This makes 30–40 biscuits, depending on the exact size of your cutter. They can be stored in an airtight container for several days or, if you want to keep them longer, you can freeze them.

If you don't have any curry powder, you can substitute it with a pinch of mustard powder to add some spice.

Marie-Christine Willis, Mummy to Alexandra, Catalina & Matthew

Salmon Pinwheels

 Kid's food   8 months   No baking

fun, quick, delicious and, better still, no baking required. Quantities are irrelevant here, make as much or a little as you wish, but you will need:

1 tin of salmon
sliced bread
butter for spreading
Philadelphia cheese

1. Cut the crusts off the bread and butter each slice.

2. Drain the salmon and mix it with enough Philadelphia to make a spreadable paste.

3. Spread fairly thinly onto the buttered bread and then roll the slices into sausage shapes.

4. Chill briefly in the fridge before cutting them into small rounds and serve for tea or as a party snack.

Justine Shenton, Mummy to Ben & Katie

Pastry Snails

 Family food   8 months   20 mins baking

Just as many children adore garlic, I haven't come across one yet that won't eat pesto. Here's a simple pesto-based idea that would make an ideal snack or savoury finger food for children's parties. It's also great for making with children, who can help to roll the pastry and mould the end of each wheel into a snail's head.

1 sheet puff pastry
1 jar green pesto
grated Parmesan cheese

1. Pre-heat the oven to 180°C (fan 160°C), 350°F, Gas Mark 4. Grate the cheese and roll out the pastry to about 5 mm (¼ inch) thick.

2. Spread the rolled pastry with pesto (you won't need the whole jar) and then sprinkle the grated Parmesan on top. Next, you need to roll up the pastry into a long sausage and cut wheels about 1 cm (½ inch) thick.

3. Lay them on a greased baking tray and manipulate the end of each wheel to make a 'snail's head'. (If you decide to do these as a canapé for adults at any stage, you can leave them as wheels.)

4. Bake them for about 20 minutes or until golden brown. Serve warm.

Phillipa Smith, Mummy to Cara

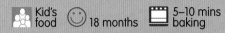

Banana and Bacon Rolls

Kid's food | 18 months | 5–10 mins baking

These are a delicious twist on 'Devils on Horseback', which are a real favourite in our house. Traditionally you make them with dates but this version using bananas is fantastically sweet and a delicious party food for kids or adults. This makes roughly 20 rolls so you may need to double the quantities for a party. I can assure you, they'll all get eaten.

10 rashers of streaky bacon
2 bananas

1 Remove the bacon rind and cut each rasher in half.

2 Cut the bananas into chunks roughly the same width as the bacon and wrap a piece of bacon around each banana chunk. It's all fairly sticky so they should hold together fairly well. Place them on a well-greased baking tray keeping the join in the bacon on the underside.

3 Grill them on full for 5–10 minutes, turning halfway through.

Allow them to cool just a little and then serve straight away.

Dodie Pryke, Mummy to India and Jamie

Happy Birthday Sandwiches

Kid's food | 12 months | No baking

This makes around 30–40 sandwiches that will look just as appealing as the cakes, sweets and other treats that might also be on the table.

4 slices wholemeal multigrain bread
4 slices wholemeal bread
4 slices white bread
110 g (4 oz) butter, softened
25 g (1 oz) cream cheese
1 heaped tablespoon crunchy peanut butter
Marmite

1 Butter the bread on 1 side only, then spread 2 slices of the multigrain bread with the cream cheese, 2 slices of the wholemeal with peanut butter and 2 of the white with Marmite.

2 Sandwich together, with the remaining buttered slices.

3 Stamp out the letters of 'Happy Birthday' and your child's name with the cutters, switching randomly between the breads so that every other sandwich in each word is different.

4 Arrange them on a large plate or colourful tray and cover until ready to serve.

You can make them the day before the birthday party and store them covered in clingfilm in the fridge.

Lorna Wing, Mummy to Charlie and food writer for *Sainsbury's Magazine*

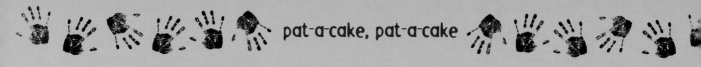

Snacks on Sticks

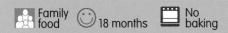 Family food ☺ 18 months No baking

This is a great idea for reluctant eaters and, if you stack your sticks with the right foods, it's possible to create an entirely balanced meal.

You can do them with whatever you have in the fridge or cupboard, making sweet or savoury kebabs or a mixture of both. Choose contrasting colours so that they look appetising and mix soft things with crunchy things for texture.

There are no 'ingredients' as such but here are just some of the foods that work well on a stick:

Baby sweetcorn; red, orange or yellow peppers which are sweeter than green; carrot; canned mandarin oranges; Cheddar cheese; salami; pineapple cubes; cherry tomatoes; strawberries; seedless grapes; baby mushrooms; small cooked beetroots; cooked frankfurter sausages; sliced ham; mozzarella cheese; pitted olives; slices of peach or nectarine.

Some ideas for building your kebabs to tempt little taste buds and please little palates are as follows:

Ham and Fruit
pineapple/pepper/mandarin orange/rolled ham/pineapple etc.

Fruity Treat
grape/peach slice/strawberry/mandarin etc.

Frankfurter and Tomato
tomato/slice of frankfurter/pineapple/pepper/sweetcorn/tomato etc.

Italian Job
mozzarella/tomato/olive/salami etc.

Just make these up as you go along, let the children create their own and, most of all, have fun.

Sheila Harris, Granny to Rachel, Andrew & Matthew

 savouries

Bacon Twists

 Family food ☺ 18 months ▭ 10–15 mins baking

These are so tasty and make great party food for children or adults.

1 pack puff pastry
1 egg
mustard powder
15–20 narrow rashers streaky bacon

1. Preheat the oven to 200°C (fan 180°C), 400°F or Gas Mark 6.

2. Children can help right from the start here by beating the egg with the mustard powder.

3. You will need about half of your pack of puff pastry (freeze the other half), which you need to roll out to about 5 mm (¼ inch) thick on a clean, floured surface. Brush the rolled sheet of pastry with the egg and then cut it into strips about 5 mm (¼ inch) wide and roughly the same length as the bacon rashers.

4. Next cook the bacon. You don't want to cook it fully at this stage as it is going to go into the oven with the pastry later. Either grill it lightly on both sides or cook it in the microwave (about 2 minutes in an 800w oven) with a piece of kitchen roll on top and underneath that will help to keep it flexible enough to twist.

5. Take one pastry strip and one rasher of bacon and twist them together. Repeat this until you run out of pastry or bacon and place them side by side on a buttered baking tray. Brush the tops of the twists with more egg.

6. Put them in the oven for 10–15 minutes, until the pastry is golden brown, and then serve warm.

You can prepare these in advance if you need to and re-heat them in an oven of the same temperature for around 5–7 minutes.

Fiona Macartney

Cheese Cubes

Family food   8 months   12–20 mins baking

Making this is a bit like making cheese fondue except that you then bake these cubes in the oven. Good fun for children but be very careful as the cheese mixture will be hot. You could use those wooden kebab sticks for dipping instead of the shorter cocktail sticks; this at least puts some distance between small hands and hot cheese sauce. This should definitely be made under a watchful eye.

75 g (3 oz) soft, full-fat cream cheese
115 g (4 oz) Cheddar cheese, coarsely grated
225 g (8 oz) softened butter
1 white loaf (unsliced)
2 egg whites

1. Preheat the oven to 190°C (fan 170°C), 375°F or Gas Mark 5. Melt the cheeses and butter together by stirring them in a mixing bowl sitting in a pan of hot water on a moderate heat.

2. While you are waiting for them to melt, slice the bread into roughly 2.5 cm (1 inch) slices, cut the crusts off and make roughly 2.5 cm (1 inch) cubes out of the slices.

3. Next, beat the egg whites until they are stiff and gently fold into the soft cheese mixture.

4. Using a cocktail or longer kebab stick, dip the bread cubes into the cheesy mixture and place them on a well-greased baking tray. Space them well so that the sides of each cube get a chance to brown nicely while baking. You can either bake them straight away for 12–20 minutes (until golden brown) or cover them with clingfilm and leave them in the fridge until you want to bake them. The cheesy mixture will inevitably spread a little on the baking tray but don't worry about this. Serve warm.

You can vary this recipe by adding any of the following to the cheese sauce:
black pepper
sun-dried tomato paste
pesto
olive tapenade
Worcestershire sauce
mustard

However, children will probably prefer them as they come.

Belinda Johnstone

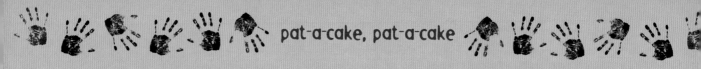

Cheese Straws

 Family food   ☺ 8 months   🗓 10–12 mins baking

This is a really traditional party savoury that children generally adore. The straws are also very easy for them to make.

225 g (8 oz) plain flour
225 g (8 oz) unsalted butter, diced and softened
170 g (6 oz) grated Cheddar cheese, the stronger the better
½–1 tsp Cayenne pepper
1 tbsp water
½ tsp salt, if desired
grated Parmesan cheese

Put all of the flour, butter, cheese and Cayenne pepper into the food processor and combine until the mixture resembles breadcrumbs.

Running the food processor on maximum, add the water until the mixture forms a big dough ball. (This could all be done by hand but anything for an easy life!)

Wrap the dough ball in clingfilm and put it in the fridge for an hour. While this is chilling, grease your baking trays and preheat the oven to 180°C (fan 160°C), 350°F or Gas Mark 4.

Once chilled, roll out the dough to about 2 cm (¾ inch) thick and cut it into around 35–45 fingers. Sprinkle with grated Parmesan and bake for 10–12 minutes. Serve warm.

Jo Perkins, Mummy to Kate & Tom

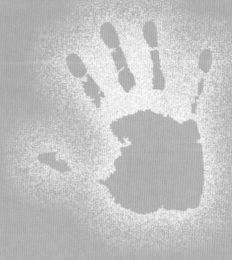

Louis's Gougères

 Family food   ☺ 8 months   ▦ 20 mins baking

These wonderful gooey cheesy pastries make fabulous party food or a tasty snack.

110 g (4 oz) plain flour
85 g (3 oz) butter
240 ml (9 fl oz) milk or water
4 large eggs, lightly beaten
110 g (4 oz) Gruyère or mature Cheddar cheese, diced into tiny cubes
salt
pepper to taste

1. Set the oven at 200°C (fan 180°C), 400°F or Gas Mark 6 and then line 2 baking trays with baking paper.

2. Sift the flour and set it aside.

3. Put the butter, milk or water, a pinch of salt and pepper to taste into the saucepan and heat slowly until the butter has melted. Raise the heat and bring it to a fast boil.

4. As soon as it is bubbling wildly, tip in the flour very quickly. Take it off the heat and beat it with an electric hand whisk until the mixture pulls away from the sides of the pan.

5. Beat in the eggs a little at a time, until the mixture is smooth and glossy. Stop once it reaches dropping consistency – you may not need all of the egg.

6. Add half of the cheese cubes to the mixture and stir until the cheese melts (you may need to pop it back on the heat for a minute).

7. Spoon the mixture onto the lined baking trays. Use about a heaped teaspoonful for each gougère, (you should get 35–45 out of this mixture). Take the remaining cheese and place a single cube in the centre of each.

8. Bake for about 20 minutes until they have puffed up and turned golden brown. Leave them on the baking trays to cool slightly and then serve warm.

Rona Stuart-Bourne, Mummy to Edward, Louis, Annabel & Marcus

Good Old Victoria Sponge

Family food   8 months   30–35 mins baking

This is simply the easiest stock sponge cake that you could hope to make. It was the first cake that I ever made with my mother and she has supplied this recipe along with a couple of great ideas for variations.

For a really traditional Victoria Sandwich:

175 g (6 oz) butter, softened
175 g (6 oz) caster sugar
3 large eggs, beaten
175 g (6 oz) self-raising flour

1. Set the oven to 170°C (fan 150°C), 325°F or Gas Mark 3 and grease and line the bases of 2 cake tins, about 18 cm (7 inches) in diameter.

2. In a mixing bowl, cream the softened butter and sugar to a pale, fluffy consistency, either with a wooden spoon or electric hand whisk.

3. Add the beaten eggs a little at a time and beat continually.

4. Sift half of the flour into the mixture and fold in well with a metal spoon. Repeat this with the remainder of the flour until you achieve a good dropping consistency.

5. Spoon half of the mixture into each cake tin, smooth with the underside of your spoon, and bake for roughly 30–35 minutes until the sponge is golden brown and springy to touch. Cool on a wire rack.

6. When both cakes are thoroughly cooled, turn them upside down and spread whipped cream onto one side and jam onto the other. Sandwich the two sides together and sift over a little icing sugar.

For a fruity sponge cake:

1. Make the basic sponge mixture and spoon the whole lot into one prepared round tin, or loaf tin.

2. Arrange one of the following evenly over the mixture:
1 large cooking apple (peeled, cored, quartered and sliced)
1 handful dried apricots
6–8 plums (pitted and sliced)
2 handfuls raspberries

3. Sprinkle the fruit with Demerara sugar and bake in a slightly hotter oven, 190°C (fan 170°C), 375°F or Gas Mark 5 for around 40 minutes.

For iced sponge fingers:

1. Grease and line the base of a rectangular or square cake tin. Spoon the basic sponge mixture into the tin, bake as for the fruity sponge cake, and turn out onto a wire rack. When the sponge has cooled thoroughly, cut it into fingers.

2. Make up some icing (whatever colour you prefer) and smooth over the top of the sponge fingers. Let your children decorate them – chocolate drops make great dominoes but any sweets or cake decorations make these ideal for serving at a children's party.

Susan Smith, Granny to George, Daisy, Edward, Tom & Lottie

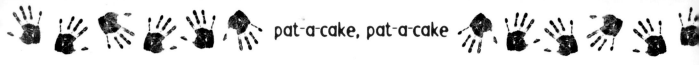

pat-a-cake, pat-a-cake

Fudgy Chocolate Layer Cake

 Family food   8 months   30–35 mins baking

A good chocolate cake is a must in all mothers' repertoires and this one makes for a delicious birthday or anything-else cake.

For the cake:
75 g (3 oz) plain chocolate, broken into pieces
200 ml (7 fl oz) milk
250 g (9 oz) dark muscovado sugar
75 g (3 oz) butter, softened
2 eggs, beaten
½ tsp vanilla essence
150 g (5½ oz) plain flour
25 g (1 oz) cocoa
1 tsp bicarbonate of soda

Icing and decoration:
100 g (3½ oz) butter, softened
200 g (7 oz) icing sugar
100 g (3½ oz) plain chocolate, melted
1 tbsp milk
grated chocolate to decorate

1. Preheat the oven to 180°C (fan 160°C), 350°F or Gas Mark 4 and grease and line the bases of 2 sandwich tins, about 20 cm (8 inches) in diameter.

2. Put the chocolate, milk and 75 g (2½ oz) – about a third – of the muscovado sugar into a saucepan. Heat gently until the chocolate and sugar have melted. Allow to cool.

3. In a large mixing bowl, beat the butter and remaining sugar together until they are creamy and really well combined. Gradually beat in the eggs, vanilla essence and the chocolate milk mixture.

4. Sift together the flour, cocoa and bicarbonate of soda. Gently fold into the cake mixture, using a figure-of-eight action to incorporate as much air as possible.

5. Turn into the prepared tins and bake for 30–35 minutes. Turn out onto a wire rack and leave to cool completely.

6. For the icing, beat the butter and sugar together. Gradually mix in the melted chocolate and milk.

7. Sandwich the cakes together with half of the icing and use the other half to ice the top. If you want to cover the sides as well, I would double the quantities suggested for the icing.

8. Decorate as you wish, letting the children take over.

Caroline Hansel, Mummy to Thomas, Daniel & Matthew

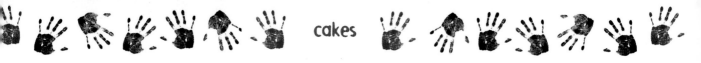

Banana Bread

 Family food ☺ 8 months 🎞 55 mins baking

I became rather obsessed with this recipe when I was pregnant with Tom, Daisy's little brother. I made it several times and learned a couple of very important lessons. Firstly, don't make banana bread when you're pregnant because you simply can't stop eating it; and secondly, the best way to eat it – particularly if it's a few days old – is to slice a piece off, warm it through in the toaster (don't toast it, just leave it in long enough to warm it) and then spread it with butter. Obviously not a calorie conscious decision but a guaranteed hit.

300 g (10½ oz) plain flour
100 g (3½ oz) granulated sugar
¾ tsp bicarbonate of soda
½ tsp salt
3 very ripe bananas, mashed with a fork
100 g (3½ oz) plain yogurt
2 large eggs, beaten lightly
90 g (3¼ oz) butter, melted and cooled
1 tsp vanilla essence

1. Grease and flour the bottom of a loaf tin then preheat your oven to 180°C (fan 160°C), 350°F, or Gas Mark 4.

2. Next, sift together the flour, sugar, bicarbonate of soda and salt in a large bowl and set it aside.

3. In another bowl, mix the mashed bananas, yogurt, beaten eggs, butter and vanilla essence with a wooden spoon. You can use a food mixer here if you wish.

4. Once these ingredients have been combined, they need to be folded into the dry ingredients with a spatula. Adult supervision is required here since over-mixing will prevent the bread from rising as it should.

5. Once you have a thick, chunky batter, scrape it into the prepared loaf tin and bake for about 55 minutes. A good test for ensuring that it has cooked through is to insert a cocktail stick into the centre of the loaf. If it comes out clean, the loaf is cooked.

6. Leave it to cool for 5 minutes in the tin and then turn it out onto a wire rack. Technically, it should then cool for slightly longer but mine rarely gets that far intact.

Sarah Rogers, Mummy to Hannah, Joe & Lily

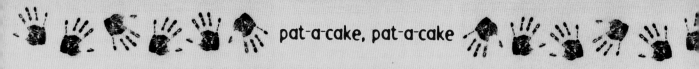

Gingerbread Sweetie House

Kid's food | 12 months | 13–15 mins baking

I can't pretend that this recipe isn't quite a commitment but the adoration that you will be able to lap up if you produce this for a birthday party will be well worth the effort.

For the gingerbread:
225 g (8 oz) butter or margarine
225 g (8 oz) black treacle
225 g (8 oz) sugar
475 g (1 lb 1 oz) plain flour
3 tsp ground ginger
1 tsp baking powder
1 tsp grated nutmeg
1 tsp salt

For the icing:
1 large egg white
185 g (6½ oz) sifted icing sugar
½ tsp cream of tartar
 (you will need to make 3 or 4 times this amount, but only make this much at a time as it sets quickly)

For decorating:
There's a whole host of cake decorations and sweets to choose from but these work really well: chocolate drops covered with hundreds & thousands – milk & white; dolly mixtures; liquorice allsorts; Smarties

1. Preheat the oven to 190°C (fan 170°C), 375°F or Gas Mark 5. Melt the butter or margarine in a saucepan over a low heat. Add the treacle and sugar and stir until the sugar fully dissolves. Remove from the heat.

2. Sift all the other gingerbread ingredients into a bowl and gradually mix all but one-fifth into the melted mixture. Form into a dough. Put on a clean and floured surface and knead in the remaining one-fifth by hand.

3. Divide the dough into 3 equal balls. Put each ball onto greaseproof paper or a greased baking sheet and roll them into rectangles 5 mm (¼ inch) thick.

4. Now you need to create the sides and roof.
Sheet 1: cut 2 rectangles for the front and back of the house about 10 x 20 cm (4 x 8 inches).
Sheet 2: cut 2 identical shapes for the sides of the house. Aim for a square with a triangle on top (about 19 cm (7 ½ inches) to highest point and 14 cm (5 ½ inches) across.
Sheet 3: cut 2 identical rectangles for the roof about 23 x 12 cm (9 x 4 ½ inches). You can trim them to fit after baking. Use the excess dough to make any decorations you like, trees, gingerbread men etc.

5. Bake in the preheated oven for 13–15 minutes until light brown. Remove from the oven, mark out a door on the front and window shapes on each of the 4 sides while it's still soft. Allow to cool completely on a wire rack, then cut out and remove the door and window shapes.

6. To mix up the first batch of icing, beat the egg white with an electric mixer in a small bowl until foamy. Gradually add the icing sugar and cream of tartar until stiff peaks form.

7. To assemble, use a cake base or a piece of thick cardboard and spread a thick icing base in which one side and either the front or back pieces will stand. Push these pieces into the icing base and press the corners together. Bulk up the inside of the corner with icing to reinforce the joint and let it stand for a few minutes. Repeat to create your 4-sided house. Let stand for at least 15 minutes.

8. Make up another icing batch. Take the 2 roof sections and place upside down on a clean flat surface, just touching where the join in the top of the roof should be. Put a thin covering of icing over both parts and cut a piece of greaseproof paper to fit across the 2 sections, slightly smaller than the roof. Let it dry for a few minutes.

9. Put a heavy bead of icing along the 2 ends of the house and place the roof (paper-side down) onto the house. Let it all stand until set.

10. Using icing as glue, stick on the decorations. Chocolate drops make great roof tiles and use liquorice allsorts for the chimney.

Zoe Brewer, Mummy to Tiger & Flame

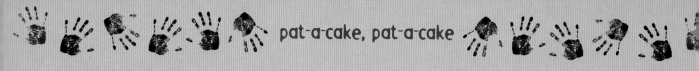

Date and Banana Loaf

 Family food   😊 8 months   🍴 60–90 mins baking

As the name suggests, this follows the banana bread theme but has a delicious twist.

250 g (9 oz) pitted dried dates
90 ml (3 fl oz) water
grated zest and juice of 1 lemon
2 ripe bananas
175 g (6 oz) unsalted butter, softened
175 g (6 oz) caster sugar
3 eggs
225 g (8 oz) self-raising flour
½ tsp baking powder
½ tsp ground cinnamon (optional)

1. Grease and flour a loaf tin and then preheat the oven to 160°C (fan 140°C), 325°F, or Gas Mark 3.

2. Set aside 4 dates and place the others in a small saucepan with the water, lemon zest and juice. Bring to the boil, reduce the heat and simmer for 5 minutes until the dates are soft and pulpy. Purée with a blender until smooth.

3. Next, mash the bananas with a fork until they also reach a smooth consistency. Children can safely do this while you are concentrating on the dates. Both of these purées should have a similar consistency. If you find that the dates are thicker, let them down with a little water. Set both of these purées aside.

4. Cream the butter and sugar in a bowl or your mixer until they are pale and fluffy. Add the banana purée and the eggs and mix together. Finally, add the flour, baking powder and cinnamon and mix until thoroughly combined.

5. Take roughly a third of this banana mixture and spoon it into your loaf tin, levelling the surface. Spread half of the date purée over the top. Repeat these layers once and then cover with the remaining banana mixture.

6. Cut the 4 remaining dates into slivers and scatter them over the surface. Bake in the preheated oven for 1–1¼ hours until the loaf is well risen and firm to the touch. Let it rest in the tin for 15 minutes and then turn it out onto a wire rack to cool.

Rona Stuart-Bourne, Mummy to Edward, Louis, Annabel & Marcus

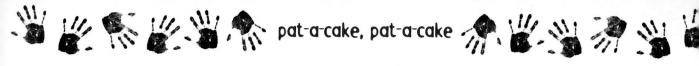
Lemon Polenta Cake

Family food   8 months   50–60 mins baking

This wonderful cake is as good served cold as a snack as it is served warm with a big dollop of cream or crème fraîche on top for pudding.

250 g (9 oz) softened butter
250 g (9 oz) sugar
250 g (9 oz) polenta
250 g (9 oz) ground almonds
4 eggs
2 lemons

1. Set the oven at 160°C (fan 140°C), 325°F or Gas Mark 3. Butter a round cake tin, about 20 cm (8 inches) and weigh out the first 4 ingredients. This is pretty uncomplicated since you need the same amount of everything and so it is very easy for a child to do with a little guidance.

2. Cream the butter and sugar together in a mixing bowl. Once the mixture is white and fluffy, add the polenta and ground almonds.

3. Add the eggs, one at a time. Keep mixing with a wooden spoon, you don't need a food processor for this, which always saves on the washing up.

4. Grate the zest of the two lemons over the bowl and then juice them and add the juice. If you think your kids might find this too lemony, forget the zest and just add the juice.

5. Spoon it all into the cake tin, smooth out and bake for 50–60 minutes. It should be golden brown on the outside but when you cut into it, you will find a wonderful lemon-yellow centre. Turn it out of its tin and cool on a wire rack.

John Nolan, Daddy to Richard, Patrick & Rosie

cakes

Cold Tea Fruit Bread

 Family food   ☺ 12 months   🎞 60 mins baking

This is one of my mother's recipes and a 'healthy' cake option. Excellent as a break time or lunch box snack.

350 g (12 oz) mixed fruit
210 ml (7½ fl oz) cold tea
115 g (4 oz) Demerara sugar
1 egg, beaten
225 g (8 oz) self-raising flour

1. Leave the fruit, tea and sugar in a covered bowl to soak over night.

2. The following morning, grease and line the base of a loaf tin and set the oven to 180°C (fan 160°C), 350°F or Gas Mark 4.

3. Using a wooden spoon, mix the beaten egg and flour into the other ingredients. Spoon into the loaf tin and bake for approximately 1 hour. Place on a wire rack to cool.

Susan Smith, Granny to George, Daisy, Edward, Tom & Lottie

Cinnamon Crumble Cake

 Family food   ☺ 8 months   🎞 35–40 mins baking

This cake offers the best of both worlds — a soft and spongy cake combined with a layer of delicious crumble.

For the cake mixture:
100 g (4 oz) margarine
2 tbsp clear honey
2 eggs, lightly beaten
100 g (4 oz) wholemeal flour

For the crumble mixture:
75 g (3 oz) margarine
75 g (3 oz) wholemeal flour
75 g (3 oz) rolled oats
50 g (2 oz) Demerara sugar
1 tsp ground cinnamon

1. Preheat the oven to 190°C (fan 170°C), 375°F or Gas Mark 5 and lightly oil a 20 cm (8 inch) cake tin.

2. To make the cake, cream the margarine and honey until light, then beat in the eggs and fold in the flour.

3. For the crumble, rub the margarine into the flour with your fingertips, then stir in the remaining ingredients.

4. Spoon half the cake mixture into the tin, then half the crumble mixture. Cover with the rest of the sponge and top with crumble.

5. Bake in the oven for 35–40 minutes until firm. Place on a wire rack to cool.

Thank you to Mornflake Oats of Cheshire for this recipe and to Daisy's Babcia for gaining permission to use it

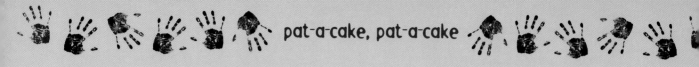

Imagination Cakes

 Kid's food   8 months 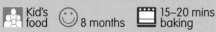 15–20 mins baking

No children's recipe book would be complete without paying homage to traditional fairy cakes. And that's exactly what these are but, on the suggestion of my godmother, I am calling them Imagination Cakes. A perfect name for individual cakes that can be 'individualised' to your heart's content. The only limit here is your child's imagination.

Base cake mix

100 g (3½ oz) butter or margarine, softened
100 g (3½ oz) caster sugar
100 g (3½ oz) self-raising flour
2 eggs, beaten

1 This makes around 8–10 fairy cakes, so either have a muffin tin ready lined with fairy cake cases or simply place 10 fairy cake cases on a baking tray (a muffin tin will produce better shaped cakes). Then preheat the oven to 190°C (fan 170°C), 375°F or Gas Mark 5.

2 Take the softened butter and sugar and cream them together in a mixing bowl until they are pale and fluffy.

3 Add the beaten eggs gradually, mixing well each time.

4 Sieve the flour into the mixture, folding it in with a wooden spoon.

5 Spoon the mixture into the paper cases, filling them about half full and bake them in the preheated oven for 15–20 minutes.

Once the cakes have cooled (on a wire rack), they need to be iced. This is where you can let your imagination take over.

For the icing

100 g (3½ oz) icing sugar
1–2 tbsp water
vanilla essence
food colouring (various colours)
sweets and cake decorations (chocolate sprinkles, silver balls, cherries, dolly mixtures, Smarties or anything else that you can think of)

1 Sieve the icing sugar into a bowl, add the water (gradually, the last thing you want is too much) and a few drops of vanilla essence, and beat the mixture into a thick, flowing consistency.

2 Add a few drops of whatever food colouring takes your fancy. If you can't decide, decant the icing into two, three or even four separate bowls and colour them all differently.

3 Spoon the icing onto the cakes and spread evenly with a knife. Decorate to your heart's content. If very young siblings will be tasting these, make sure that any toppings are appropriate for them.

Biddy Robertson, Mummy to James & Mark

It's great to watch girls and boys do their own thing with fairy cakes. Without wishing to create stereotypes, girls generally plump for pink and pretty whereas boys tend towards bright primary colours. Here are a couple of ideas that might appeal more to either girls or boys:

Butterfly Cakes for Little Princesses

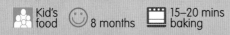

Kid's food   8 months   15–20 mins baking

Make the basic fairy cakes as described on page 146. When they have cooled, cut across the top of each cake with a sharp knife and then halve the bit that you have chopped off the top.

You then need to make butter icing to heap fairly generously on top of each cake before replacing your two 'butterfly wings'.

75 g (3 oz) butter, softened
175 g (6 oz) icing sugar
vanilla essence
1–2 tbsp warm water
food colouring (preferably red, which makes pink butter icing)

Cream the butter in a bowl until it is soft. Sieve the icing sugar onto the butter and add a few drops of vanilla essence. Stir in the water gradually to achieve a thick, 'heapable' consistency. Colour as you wish, put a generous dollop on top of each fairy cake and then crown them with their butterfly wings.

Mark & Becky Rubens, Parents to Isabel, Tabitha & Gabriel

Lairy Cakes for Bullish Boys

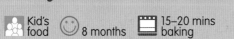

Kid's food   8 months   15–20 mins baking

Make the basic fairy cakes as described on page 146. Before spooning the mixture into the paper cases, take another mixing bowl and halve the mixture. Add a few drops of red food colouring to one and a few drops of green food colouring to the other.

Spoon the mixture into the fairy cake cases, putting a little red and a little green into each case. Bake the lairy cakes for 15–20 minutes.

Once they have cooled, ice them using the basic icing but add some bright blue food colouring. Once decorated, these are good enough for any self-respecting boy.

Sarah Myers, Mummy to Charlie

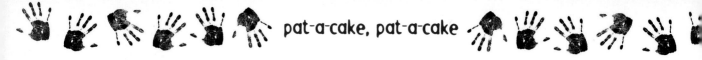

pat-a-cake, pat-a-cake

Strawberry Buns

 Kid's food   😊 8 months   🗔 12–15 mins baking

This recipe for these delicious bready and almost scone-like buns comes from the television presenter, Wendy Turner Webster. She makes these with her little boy, Jack, who apparently has a particular penchant for the jammy centres.

225 g (8 oz) wholemeal flour
1½ tsp baking power
25 g (1 oz) margarine
25 g (1 oz) caster sugar
150 ml (5 fl oz) whole milk
4 tbsp strawberry jam (or any jam of your choice)

1. Preheat the oven to 200°C (fan 180°C), 400°F, Gas Mark 6 and grease a baking tray.

2. Sift the flour and baking powder into a bowl. Rub in the margarine until the mixture resembles fine breadcrumbs.

3. Add the sugar then the milk and mix into a dough. Knead the dough on a lightly floured board until it is smooth.

4. With floured hands, roll into 6–8 balls and place them on a greased baking tray, well spaced apart. Make little holes in the centre of each bun and fill with the jam.

5. Bake for about 12–15 minutes until risen and slightly browned. Allow them to cool off slightly on the baking tray and then transfer them to a wire rack.

Wendy Turner Webster, Mummy to Jack

Chocolate Muffins with Orange and Allspice

Family food   12 months   15 mins baking

This muffin recipe was sent to me by Clare Gordon-Smith, author of the wonderful *Flavouring with...* series of cook books. This is from *Flavouring with Spices*, published by Ryland, Peters & Small.

These muffins are great for breakfast or as a pudding or snack.

250 g (9 oz) plain flour
1 tbsp baking powder
½ tsp bicarbonate of soda
2 tbsp cocoa powder
75 g (3 oz) soft brown sugar
½ tsp ground allspice
50 g (2 oz) plain dark chocolate
grated rind of 1 orange
1 egg
250 ml (9 fl oz) whole milk

1. Preheat your oven to 200°C (fan 180°C), 400°F or Gas Mark 6.

2. Place 9 muffin cases in a bun tray.

3. Put the flour, baking powder, bicarbonate of soda, cocoa powder, brown sugar and allspice in a bowl.

4. Break the chocolate into small pieces and stir it into the bowl together with the orange rind.

5. Beat the egg and milk together until well blended (do not over mix), then fold into the dry ingredients.

6. Divide the mixture between the muffin cases and bake for 15 minutes, or until risen and firm to the touch. Cool on a wire rack.

Mini Passion Fruit Cakes

Family food | 18 months | 15 mins baking

Delicious, healthy, tiny cupcakes.

85 g (3 oz) butter
115 g (4 oz) caster sugar
140 g (5 oz) self-raising flour, sifted
1 egg and 1 egg yolk
pulp of 2 passion fruits

1. Preheat the oven to 180°C (fan 160°C), 350°F or Gas Mark 4 and set out around 20–25 truffle or mini muffin cases on a baking tray or, for best results, in mini muffin tins.

2. Cream the butter and sugar in a mixing bowl until pale, by hand or with an electric whisk.

3. Beat in the egg and extra yolk until pale and fluffy.

4. Stir in the passion fruit pulp (if you're unfamiliar with passion fruit, don't be put off by the seeds – it's all delicious). Then, bit by bit, add the flour and mix in thoroughly.

5. Spoon into truffle cases and bake for 15 minutes or until golden at the edges. Cool on a wire rack.

6. Either sprinkle with sifted icing sugar, or ice with coloured icing, then sprinkle with hundreds and thousands or chocolate vermicelli.

Sonya Szpojnarowicz, Mummy to Max, Lukas, Jakob and Kaspar

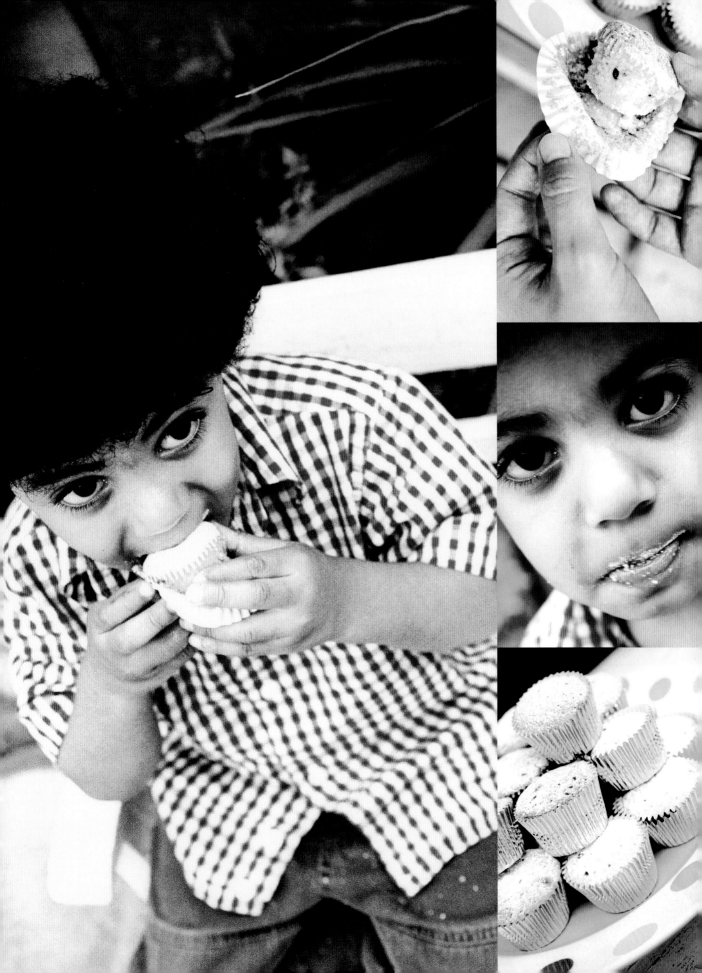

Strawberry Cheesecake Muffins

 Family food   ☺ 8 months   15 mins baking

This recipe was kindly sent to me by the presenter and food writer, Silvana Franco. I think the combination of these two favourite treats is too much to resist.

For the muffin:

200 g (7 oz) plain flour
1 tbsp baking powder
½ tsp salt
75 g (3 oz) caster sugar
grated rind of 1 large orange
1 egg
200 ml (7 fl oz) whole milk
50 g (2 oz) butter, melted

For the filling:

100 g (3½ oz) soft cheese
2 tbsp caster sugar
6 strawberries, halved

1. Preheat the oven to 200°C (fan 180°C), 400°F or Gas Mark 6 and set out 12 muffin cases, either in a muffin tin or on a baking tray.

2. Sieve the flour and baking powder into a large bowl then stir in the salt, sugar and orange rind.

3. Beat the egg and milk together in a jug or bowl and roughly mix into the dry ingredients with the butter to make a loose, slightly lumpy mixture.

4. Mix together the soft cheese and sugar. Half-fill the 12 paper muffin cases with about two-thirds of the muffin mixture then push half a strawberry into each. Top with a teaspoon of the sugary cheese then spoon over the remaining muffin mixture to cover.

5. Bake for 15 minutes until well risen and cracked and browned on top. Remove from the tin and cool on a wire rack.

If you don't devour them all at once, pack them into an airtight cake tin for storage.

Carrot and Apple Bite-Sized Muffins

Family food · 8 months · 20–25 mins baking

The inspiration for these came from an Annabel Karmel recipe. They make tiny, healthy treats for children from as young as 8 months. The following makes around 45 bite-sized muffins. It's not hard to eat three at a time so they won't last as long as you might think.

85 g (3 oz) grated carrots
2 apples, peeled and grated
120 ml (4 fl oz) vegetable oil
3 eggs lightly beaten
50 g (2 oz) soft brown sugar
50 g (2 oz) caster sugar
1 tsp vanilla essence

85 g (3 oz) wholemeal flour
100 g (3½ oz) self-raising flour
1 tbsp baking powder
½ tsp bicarbonate of soda
½ tsp salt
½ tsp ground cinnamon
½ tsp ground ginger
75 g (2½–3 oz) currants

1. Preheat the oven to 180°C (fan 160°C), 350°F or Gas Mark 4 and cover 2 baking trays with truffle or mini muffin cases.

2. Peel and grate the carrot and apples and then mix them together with the oil, eggs, soft brown and caster sugars and vanilla essence in a large bowl. You will be left with a sloppy, oily mixture that should now be set aside for a moment.

3. Sift all the dry ingredients together (except the currants) in another bowl. When you sift the wholemeal flour, you will find that some of the 'wholemeal-ness' gets left in the sieve. Tip this in afterwards, don't discard it, you will at least have incorporated as much air into the mix as possible by sieving it.

4. Add this dry flour mixture to the wet mixture a little at a time and fold it in. Try not to over mix.

5. Fold in the currants.

6. Teaspoon the mixture into the tiny paper cases and bake for 20–25 minutes until they have browned nicely. Cool on a wire rack.

These store well in an airtight container.

Roz Edwards, Mummy to Chloe

Cherry Buns

 Family food 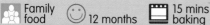 12 months 15 mins baking

This recipe is in memory of Edward Geffen who adored making these buns with his Mummy.

125 g (4½ oz) self-raising flour, sifted
1 level tsp baking powder
125 g (4½ oz) softened butter or margarine
2 eggs
125 g (4½ oz) caster sugar
60 g (2¼ oz) glacé cherries
7 extra cherries to cut in half for decoration

1. Preheat the oven to 180°C (fan 160°C), 350°F or Gas Mark 4 and have your little one set out 14 paper bun cases. The buns keep their shape best if you put the cases in a muffin tin but, if you don't have one, use a baking tray.

2. Cream together the butter and sugar in a food processor.

3. Beat the eggs in a separate bowl and chop the cherries into rough quarters (small people can do this with blunt-ended children's scissors since the cherries don't have to be cut neatly).

4. Add a little of the flour to the creamed sugar and butter in the food processor and mix in. Next mix in the beaten egg and then the rest of the flour and baking powder.

5. Remove the mixture from the food processor and fold in the cherries.

6. Put about a dessertspoon of mixture into each paper case and bake for about 15 minutes or until the buns spring back when pressed lightly. Cool on a wire rack.

7. Sieve some icing sugar onto the top of each bun and decorate with half a cherry.

Camilla Geffen, Mummy to Edward, William and Harry

Lighthouse Bakery Chocolate Chip, Oatmeal and Walnut Cookies

 Family food   😊 12 months   🗔 10–15 mins baking

The Lighthouse Bakery is, as far as I'm concerned, one of the best bakers in London. Daisy thought so too and this recipe that they have kindly contributed was one of her favourites. Now that I have the recipe, the temptation is too much to bear. This makes around 10-12 large cookies. Just be warned that once made, you will not be able to leave them alone!

115 g (4 oz) unsalted butter, softened
100 g (3½ oz) caster sugar
120 g (4½ oz) brown sugar
1 tbsp milk
1 tsp vanilla essence
1 large egg
150 g (5½ oz) plain flour
1 tsp baking powder
1 tsp bicarbonate of soda
½ tsp salt
100 g (3½ oz) porridge oats
175 g (6 oz) chocolate chips
75 g (3 oz) chopped walnuts

1. Once the butter has softened slightly, put it in the mixer with the 2 sugars and cream them until they are light and fluffy.

2. Combine the milk, vanilla essence and the egg and add them to the butter and sugar mixture. Sift in the flour, baking powder, bicarbonate of soda and salt and mix until you have your basic dough.

3. Take this out of the mixer and stir in the oats, chocolate chips and chopped walnuts with a wooden spoon. Now use your hands, as well as any little helping hands, to form cookies to whatever size you prefer (Lighthouse make big American-style cookies). This is where kids can really get involved. Place them on a well-greased baking tray leaving space for them to spread.

4. You then need to chill the cookies for at least an hour in the fridge before baking. Best results are achieved if they are left overnight but I find that the patience of small chefs doesn't always run to this. When they have chilled for as long as you can manage, heat your oven to 180°C (fan 160°C), 350°F or Gas Mark 4 and bake for 10–15 minutes. Cool on a wire rack before indulging.

Many thanks to The Lighthouse Bakery, Northcote Road, London, SW11 and to Daisy's nanny and best friend, Joanna Beme, for gaining permission to use it

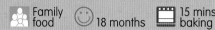

Chocolate Almond Crunchies

Family food · 18 months · 15 mins baking

A huge thank you to Delia Smith for donating this, one of her favourite biscuit recipes. 'Although you can now buy really good-quality biscuits and American cookies, making them at home still has the edge, and as biscuits are so easy, it's a very good place to start if you are a beginner in home baking. I've used "adult" chocolate in these, but for children, chocolate chips would do fine.'

(2 oz) 50 g dark continental chocolate (75% cocoa)
(4 oz) 110 g butter
(3 oz) 75 g demerara sugar
1 dessertspoon golden syrup
(1½ oz) 40 g whole almonds, unblanched
(4 oz) 110 g self-raising flour
pinch of salt
(4 oz) 110 g porridge oats

1. You will also need two baking sheets measuring (14 x 11 inches) 35 x 28 cm, lightly greased with groundnut or another flavourless oil.

2. Preheat the oven to 170°C (fan 150°C), 325°F or Gas Mark 3.

3. First of all, using a sharp knife, chop the chocolate into small chunks about (¼ inch) 5 mm square. Now put the butter, sugar and syrup in a saucepan, place it on the gentlest heat possible and let it all dissolve, which will take 2–3 minutes. Meanwhile, chop the nuts into small chunks about the same size as the chocolate pieces. When the butter mixture has dissolved, take it off the heat. In a large mixing bowl, sift in the flour and salt and add the porridge oats and half the chocolate and nuts, then give this a quick mix before pouring in the butter mixture. Now, using a wooden spoon, stir and mix everything together, then switch from a spoon to your hands to bring everything together to form a dough. If it seems a bit dry, add a few drops of cold water.

4. Now take half the dough and divide it into nine lumps the size of a large walnut, then roll them into rounds using the flat of your hand. Place them on a worktop and press gently to flatten them out into rounds, approximately (2½ inches) 6 cm in diameter, then scatter half the remaining chocolate and almonds on top of the biscuits, pressing them down lightly. Once you have filled one tray (give them enough room to spread out during baking), bake them on the middle shelf of the oven for 15 minutes whilst you prepare the second tray. When they're all cooked, leave them to cool on the baking sheets for 10 minutes, then transfer them to a wire rack to finish cooling. You could store the biscuits in a sealed container, but I doubt you'll have any left!

Crunchie variations

For Apricot Pecan Crunchies, use (2 oz) 50 g of dried apricots and (1½ oz) 40 g of pecans, chopped, instead of the chocolate and almonds.

For Cherry and Flaked-Almond Crunchies, use (2 oz) 50 g of dried sour cherries and (1½ oz) 40 g of flaked almonds.

For Raisin Hazelnut Crunchies, use (2 oz) 50 g of raisins and (1½ oz) 40 g of hazelnuts.

Copyright Delia Smith 1998 – Recipe reproduced by permission from *Delia's How to Cook Book One* (published by BBC Worldwide)

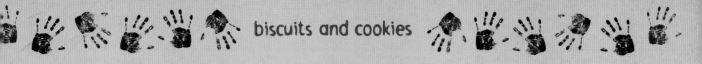

Iced Spicy Biscuits

 Kid's food ☺ 8 months 10–15 mins baking

The spicy-ness is provided by the cinnamon that gives these biscuits an adorable flavour. Ice if you like (that's the really fun bit), but they are delicious anyway.

For the biscuits:
275 g (9¾ oz) plain flour
1 level tsp baking powder
1 dessertspoon cinnamon
100 g (3½ oz) soft brown sugar
75 g (2½ oz) butter, slightly softened
1 small egg
50 g (1¾ oz) golden syrup

For the icing:
100 g (3½ oz) icing sugar
1 tbsp hot water
25 g (1 oz) cocoa powder (for chocolate icing only)
decorative toppings, eg. Smarties, cherries, chocolate drops...

1. Sift the flour, baking powder and cinnamon into a mixing bowl. Stir in the sugar.

2. Cube the butter and add it to the mixing bowl. Rub the flour, sugar and butter together with your fingertips until the mixture looks like breadcrumbs.

3. Break the egg into a jug and beat it with a fork. Then add the syrup and mix it with the egg until smooth. Make a hollow in the 'breadcrumbs' and pour in the egg mixture. Mix everything together well until you have a big ball of dough. Put in a plastic bag and chill in the fridge for half an hour.

4. Preheat the oven to 170°C (fan 150°C), 325°F or Gas Mark 3 and roll out the dough on a floured surface to about 5 mm (¼ inch) thick. Use biscuit cutters to make different shaped biscuits. You will get around 20–25 biscuits from this dough.

5. Place on greased baking trays and bake for 10–15 minutes. Cool thoroughly on a wire rack before icing.

6. Sift the icing sugar into a small bowl. Add the water, a little at a time, to make a smooth paste. For chocolate icing, use 75 g (2½ oz) icing sugar and the 25 g (1 oz) cocoa powder.

7. Spoon a little icing onto each biscuit and spread it out evenly with a wet knife. Decorate and leave the icing to set before devouring.

Just like Stained Glass Biscuits (see page 166), these make wonderful Christmas tree decorations. Make a little hole near the edge of each biscuit before baking and then, once iced, thread a thin red ribbon through each to tie them to the tree. The cinnamon gives them a very Christmassy flavour too.

Carolyn Gentle, Mummy to Peter, Michael, Edmund and Benjamin

Squidgy Banana Cookies

Kid's food   😊 8 months   🔲 10–15 mins baking

These are real short cut cookies, you don't even have to make a dough. You simply use the bananas to bind everything together. Quantities can depend on how many brown bananas you have, but the following makes 6–8 cookies. Because these are so soft they can even be appreciated by toothless wonders. For children over 12 months, you can add honey for extra sweetness.

2 overripe bananas
100 g (3½ oz) rolled oats
handful of raisins
½ tsp ground ginger
½ tsp cinnamon

1. Preheat the oven to 200°C (fan 180°C), 400°F or Gas Mark 6.

2. Mash the bananas and combine all of the other ingredients into them to form a doughy mixture.

3. Using your hands, shape as many round cookies as you can onto a greased baking sheet and flatten them slightly.

4. Bake for about 10–15 minutes until they are golden and dry on top but chewy in the middle. Let them cool on a wire rack before tucking in.

Bee Trim, Mummy to Jasper & Rohanna

Wholemeal Ginger Biscuits

Family food   😊 12 months   🔲 12–15 mins baking

A quick and easy-to-make biscuit, it feels a whole lot healthier than any shop-bought variety.

115 g (4 oz) margarine or butter
1 tbsp golden syrup
55 g (2 oz) sugar (white for crunchy biscuits or brown for softer biscuits, whichever you prefer)
175 g (6 oz) wholemeal flour
¼ tsp bicarbonate of soda
½ –1 tsp ground ginger

1. Preheat the oven to 190 °C (fan 170°C), 375°F or Gas Mark 5.

2. Melt the butter and syrup together in a pan or the microwave. Then add all the other ingredients and mix to form a doughy consistency.

3. When the mixture is cool enough, separate it into around 20–25 small dollops and roll into mini footballs (roughly the size of a 2p piece). Place them on a greased baking tray. Allow room between each one for the dough to spread. Take a teaspoon and gently flatten the balls into mini pancakes.

4. Bake in the oven for 12–15 minutes and then cool on a wire rack.

Jenny Halstein, Mummy to Andrew and Jack

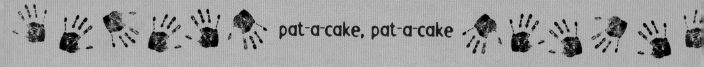
Very Yummy Chocolate Chip Cookies

 Family food
 12 months
 10–12 mins baking

Nothing compares to homemade cookies, straight from the oven so the chocolate is all warm and gooey. You can of course buy chocolate chips in packets but it's much more fun to cut the chocolate up by hand. Tastes better too.

These are chocolate cookies with gooey white chocolate chunks but if you prefer you can leave out the cocoa and make the cookies with chunks of dark chocolate.

125 g (4½ oz) luxury Belgian white chocolate
125 g (4½ oz) spreadable butter or softened butter
75 g (3 oz) soft light brown sugar
50 g (2 oz) golden granulated sugar
1 large egg
½ tsp vanilla essence
165 g (5½ oz) plain flour
1 rounded tbsp cocoa powder (about 10 g/½ oz)
¼ tsp salt
½ tsp bicarbonate of soda

This makes about 25–35 cookies (depending on how large you make them) so you will need 3 or 4 lightly greased baking trays – or use 2 twice.

1. Preheat the oven to 180°C, (fan 160°C), 350°F or Gas Mark 4.

2. Break the chocolate into chunks then cut it into smaller chips with a knife. Older kids can use an ordinary table knife to do this.

3. Cream the butter and both sugars together in a large bowl.

4. In another bowl, lightly beat the egg, add the vanilla essence then add it to the creamed butter mixture bit by bit, beating all the time.

5. Mix in the flour, cocoa, salt and bicarbonate of soda. Finally, add the chopped chocolate.

6. Drop 8–9 teaspoons of the mixture on each baking tray, leaving plenty of space in between each spoonful. Bake for 10–12 minutes until browned.

7. Remove the baking trays from the oven, leave for a couple of minutes then prise off the cookies with a palate knife and transfer them to a cooling rack.

Best served straight from the oven, on their own or with vanilla ice cream.

This recipe was sent to me by Fiona Beckett who writes regularly for *The Times*, *The Guardian* and for *Sainsbury's Magazine*.

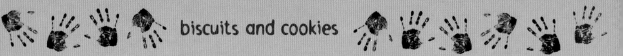

Peanut Butter Biscuits

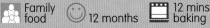 Family food   😊 12 months   🎞 12 mins baking

Peanut butter gives biscuits a delicious flavour and children will love rolling the dough into balls and then pressing them out with a fork. Obviously avoid these if there's any suspicion of nut allergy in the family.

100 g (3½ oz) butter
100 g (3½ oz) peanut butter, crunchy or smooth
½ tsp vanilla essence
100 g (3½ oz) granulated sugar
75 g (3 oz) brown sugar
1 egg
200 g (7 oz) self-raising flour
¾ tsp bicarbonate of soda
¼ tsp baking powder
extra granulated sugar for rolling

1. Preheat your oven to 190°C (fan 170°C), 375°F or Gas Mark 5.

2. In a mixing bowl, cream together the butter, peanut butter, vanilla essence, both sugars and the egg.

3. Sift the flour, bicarbonate of soda and baking powder together and stir into the mixture.

4. Roll into 2.5 cm (1 inch) balls (you will get around 20 balls out of this dough), then roll each ball into some extra granulated sugar and place on an ungreased baking tray, about 5 cm (2 inches) apart. Press down each ball with a fork dipped in hot water.

5. Bake for about 12 minutes and allow to cool a little before placing them on a wire rack to cool thoroughly.

Sue Macartney, Mummy to Fiona, Alistair & James

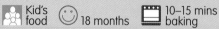

Stained Glass Biscuits

👐 Kid's food   🙂 18 months   🔲 10–15 mins baking

Boiled sweets make wonderful sugary, crunchy centres for these delicious biscuits.

225 g (8 oz) flour
½ tsp ground mixed spice
100 g (3½ oz) butter, softened
100 g (3½ oz) caster sugar
1 tbsp whole milk
10–12 boiled sweets (various colours)

Sift the flour and mixed spice into a mixing bowl.

Chop the softened butter into small cubes and rub it into the flour using your fingers until the mixture resembles breadcrumbs. Add the sugar and mix well.

Add the milk bit by bit (you may need a little more or a little less) and knead it into a soft dough. Wrap the dough in clingfilm and put it in the fridge for about 15 minutes. Set the oven to 180°C (fan 160°C), 350°F or Gas Mark 4 and grease a couple of baking trays.

Dust a surface with flour and roll the dough out to a depth of about 8 mm (⅜ inch). Cut out the biscuits using whatever shaped cutters you like and place them on the baking trays.

Using a very small round cutter (about 1.5 cm/¾ inch in diameter) or a knife, cut out holes in the centre of each biscuit. Place a boiled sweet into each hole.

Bake in the oven for about 10–15 minutes until the biscuits are golden brown around the edges and the sweets have melted. You need to leave them on the baking tray until the sweets have set a little again, then move them onto a wire rack to cool thoroughly.

As well as being delicious to eat, these biscuits look wonderful as Christmas tree decorations. Use a star-shaped cutter, make a hole at the top of each biscuit once they are cool and thread thin coloured ribbon through to hang them.

Another variation is to make traffic light biscuits using exactly the same method but to make bigger biscuits with bigger holes and place a red, green and orange sweet in each biscuit.

Caroline Imi, Mummy to Isabella & Edward

Yum Yums

 Kid's food   ☺ 8 months   📷 20–25 mins baking

Quite simply, they are as the title suggests...

225 g (8 oz) soft margarine
175 g (6 oz) caster sugar
1 egg, beaten
275 g (9¾ oz) self-raising flour
50 g (2 oz) cornflakes, lightly crushed

1. Heat the oven to 190°C (fan 170°C), 375°F or Gas Mark 5 and grease 4 large baking trays (or use 2 twice).

2. Put the margarine into a large bowl, add the sugar and beat together with a wooden spoon until soft.

3. Beat in the egg, then slowly work in the flour until the mixture has come together. Wrap it in clingfilm and chill in the fridge for 10 minutes.

4. Wet your hands, as well as those of any little ones, and lightly roll the mixture into about 30–35 balls. Then roll each one in the crushed cornflakes. Place them on the baking trays, spacing them well, and slightly flatten each ball with your hand.

5. Bake for about 20–25 minutes until they are turning a very pale brown at the edges. Remove from the oven and leave on the trays for a minute before carefully lifting each biscuit onto a wire cooling rack.

When quite cold, store in an airtight tin.

Gillian Loveridge, Granny to Isabelle, Max, Ella & Melia

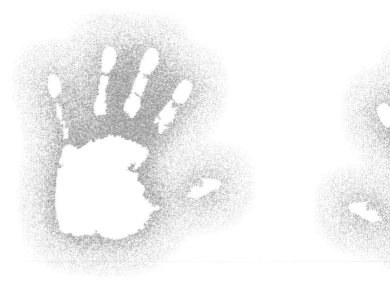

Butter Cut-Out Biscuits

Kid's food · 8 months · 8–12 mins baking

Nigella Lawson very kindly sent me this recipe. It is taken from her book, *How To Be A Domestic Goddess*, published by Chatto and Windus. What Nigella doesn't know is that the picture of Daisy on the inside back cover of this book was taken while she was making the very same biscuits using left-over dough from her first birthday preparations. Nigella says she's made these biscuits for both her children every birthday since they could eat proper food and have gone through all the stages of Barbie pink to cool blue. And although they love to have the biscuits because it's part of their birthday ritual, the bit they really like is licking off the icing!

'Like all doughs, it freezes well, so it makes sense – in a smug, domestic kind of a way – to wrap half of this in clingfilm and stash it in the deep freeze until next needed. It's hard to specify exactly how much icing you'll need, but you might end up using more than specified below if you're using a lot of different colours. I always cut out the newly acquired age of the child on his or her birthday. My children couldn't contemplate a birthday party without them.'

This makes 50–60 biscuits.

175 g (6 oz) soft unsalted butter
200 g (7 oz) caster sugar
2 large eggs
1 tsp vanilla essence
400 g (14 oz) plain flour
1 tsp baking powder
1 tsp salt
300 g (10½ oz) icing sugar, sifted, and food colouring
biscuit cutters

1. Preheat the oven to 180°C (fan 160°C), 350°F or Gas Mark 4 and grease 2 baking sheets.

2. Cream the butter and sugar together until pale and moving towards moussiness, then beat in the eggs and vanilla. In another bowl, combine the flour, baking powder and salt. Add the dry ingredients to the butter and eggs, and mix gently but surely. If you think the finished mixture is too sticky to be rolled out, add more flour, but do so sparingly as too much will make the dough tough. Halve the dough, form into fat discs, wrap each half in clingfilm and rest in the fridge for at least 1 hour. Sprinkle a suitable surface with flour, place a disc of dough on it (not taking out the other half until you've finished with the first) and sprinkle a little more flour on top of that. Then roll it out to a thickness of about 5 mm (¼ inch). Cut into shapes, dipping the cutter into flour as you go, and place the biscuits a little apart on the baking sheets.

3. Bake for 8–12 minutes, by which time they will be lightly golden around the edges. Cool on a rack and continue with the rest of the dough. When they're all fully cooled, you can get on with the icing. Put a couple of tablespoons of just-not-boiling water into a large bowl, add the sifted icing sugar and mix together, adding more water as you need to form a thick paste. Colour as desired: let the artistic spirit within you speak, remembering with gratitude that children have very bad taste.

Nigella Lawson, Mummy to Cosima & Bruno

Happy Faces

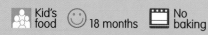 Kid's food | 18 months | No baking

It would be stretching the bounds of anyone's imagination to call this a recipe. However, it is a great way to entertain children in the kitchen and, for that, it gets my vote. Guaranteed to fill at least half an hour on a rainy afternoon as long as you can cope with the sugar rush!

1 packet of plain biscuits such as Rich Tea
several tubes of ready-made icing in different colours
2–3 packets of sweets (Smarties, Jelly Tots, dolly mixtures etc. all work well)

No explanation needed, just let your children's imaginations go to town.

This gives them a real opportunity to be creative and tests their co-ordination at the same time. You'll notice a big difference in the outcome of this culinary project as children get older. Younger children may well just end up with a pile of icing on a biscuit, while children from around four onwards should be able to make great faces or anything else that appeals to their imagination.

If you've got time and you're feeling in a baking frame of mind, try Nigella's delicious Butter Cut-Out Biscuits on page 169. That is how it should be done, but there's no harm cheating from time to time.

Sarah Gordon, Mummy to Madeleine & George

Reindeer

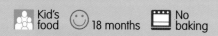 Kid's food | 18 months | No baking

Another no-bake biscuit idea that is ideal for Christmas parties or even to leave by the chimney for Father Christmas and his reindeer.

1 packet chocolate digestives
1 packet mini marshmallows
1 tube Smarties (red, yellow and green)
3 or 4 Curly Wurly bars
icing in a tube

Using the icing as glue, place a marshmallow in the centre of the chocolate covered side of the biscuit for a nose. Add two eyes with either the yellow or green smarties. Finally cut the Curly Wurlies in half widthways and lengthways and use 2 pieces to glue on for the horns.

Diana Carter, Granny to Ben & Beth

Traditional Jam Tarts

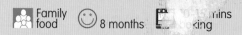 Family food   😊 8 months   ⬜ mins king

Jam tarts were one of Daisy's all time favourites, although I'm slightly ashamed to say that hers nearly always came from the supermarket. The greatest thrill of all was to devour one in the supermarket trolley while shopping. These are far superior and will be an almost guaranteed hit since I have never met a child that doesn't adore the sweet stickiness of strawberry jam.

You can buy very good shortcrust pastry and simply follow the instructions on the pack but it is much more satisfying to make it if you've got time.

For the pastry:
200 g (7 oz) flour
100 g (3½ oz) butter, softened
1 egg yolk, beaten
2 tsp caster sugar
salt

For the filling:
strawberry (or your favourite) jam

1. Sift the flour into a bowl and stir in the sugar and a pinch of salt.

2. Cube the softened butter and add it to the flour mix. Rub it in with your fingers until the mixture resembles fine breadcrumbs.

3. Add just enough very cold water to bring the breadcrumbs together to form a ball of dough. Again, this is best done with your hands. To make good pastry you should try to get the dough to form with the minimum amount of movement so gently discourage over-enthusiastic helping hands. You may need a little more water but only add just enough to make a smooth ball.

4. Wrap the pastry in clingfilm and put it in the fridge to chill for at least 30 minutes. Towards the end of this time, set your oven to 180°C (fan 160°C), 350°F or Gas Mark 4.

5. Lightly dust a smooth surface and a rolling pin with flour and roll out the pastry. Butter a tart tin (its cups are shallower than your average muffin tin) and, taking a circular pastry cutter that fits your tin's cups, cut out as many pastry circles as you can. Place them carefully in the tin's cups and brush each one lightly with a little beaten egg yolk.

6. Put a dollop (not too big or it could overflow while cooking) of your favourite jam in the middle of the pastry. Bake for around 10–15 minutes until the pastry is golden brown and the jam is all gooey. Cool on a wire rack before tucking in because the jam does get very hot.

Sarah Kerr, Mummy to Isabel, Natasha & Imogen

 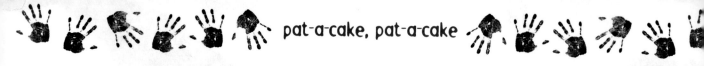

Lily Diggle's Fudge

Family food   12 months   10 mins cooking

This is a fudge recipe that has been handed down through generations. It was originally called Grandma's Fudge but I happen to know that the grandmother concerned was called Lily Diggle and I feel very strongly that such a fabulous name has to live on alongside her fudge recipe.

397 g can condensed milk
225 g (8 oz) caster sugar
55 g (2 oz) butter
2 tbsp golden syrup
vanilla essence

1. Let children weigh out all of the ingredients but make sure that an adult is firmly in charge after that since this gets very hot before it turns into fudge.

2. Take a large, heavy-based saucepan and simply mix all the ingredients (except the vanilla essence) together over a moderate heat, stirring constantly until the sugar is dissolved. DON'T let it boil yet.

3. Once the sugar grains have completely melted, turn the heat right up and boil it rapidly for 5–7 minutes, stirring all the time.

4. Then turn the heat off and, when the fudge has had the chance to cool down a little, add a few drops of vanilla essence.

5. Pour into a well-buttered flat tin and chill in the fridge for at least 5 minutes. When it has chilled, cut it into around 20 cubes. Remember fudge is very sugary and rich so don't make these too big.

Lucy & Tim Myatt, parents to Olivia & Jemima

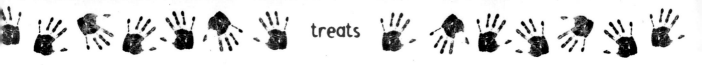
Sticky Fried Goo-Goo Cake

 Kid's food   😊 18 months   🍳 10–15 mins cooking

As the name suggests, this is a particularly sticky and gooey rice crispy cake. A toffee-flavoured twist on a more traditional Rice Crispies cake. Utterly irresistible!

115 g (4 oz) butter
115 g (4 oz) marshmallows
115 g (4 oz) plain toffee
115 g (4 oz) Rice Crispies

1. Begin by preparing all of the ingredients, allowing your children to be really hands-on with the scales.

2. Melt the butter in a fairly large saucepan on a low heat. When the butter has turned to liquid, add the marshmallows and toffee and ensure that your ring is on the lowest heat. Whatever you do, don't let it boil as you will end up with very hard and sticky fried goo-goo, which is extremely tricky for little teeth.

3. Once this mixture turns entirely to liquid, add the Rice Crispies and stir with a wooden spoon to cover them with 'goo'.

4. Put the mixture in a well-buttered dish or baking tray that needs to be around 5–8 cm (2–3 inches) deep and place it in the fridge to harden slightly. This should take about 45 minutes, at which point you should cut it into chunks or slices. Store in an airtight container in the fridge.

Nini Markes, Mummy to Araminta, Dominic, Gerard & Sylvie

Tarts with a Difference

 Kid's food   😊 12 months   🍳 15 mins baking

These are based on classic jam tarts but are much less trouble as there is no pastry involved.

slices of thinly sliced white bread
butter for spreading
jam, mincemeat or any other suitable filling

1. Preheat the oven to 180°C (fan 160°C), 350°F or Gas Mark 4.

2. Cut circles from the bread large enough to line the cups of a tart or muffin tin and flatten them very slightly with a rolling pin.

3. Butter one side of each circle with softened butter. Line the tins with the buttered bread – buttered side down.

4. Half fill each one with jam or mincemeat and bake for approximately 15 minutes. Cool on a wire rack and remember that the jam gets very hot so don't tuck in until you know they are cool.

Try these with a savoury filling such as tuna & sweetcorn, or finely chopped and sautéed bacon and mushrooms. Cover them with grated cheese for the last 5–6 minutes of cooking time.

Gill Cozens, Granny to Georgina, George & Edward

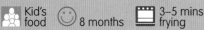

Pancakes

 Kid's food   😊 8 months   🎞 3–5 mins frying

Of course pancakes don't need to be a treat at all. There are umpteen ways to serve traditional pancakes – rolled up with easy-to-roll savoury fillings such as tuna and sweetcorn; flat and folded with sliced savoury fillings such as ham and cheese; with fresh fruit, syrup, jam or ice cream for pudding; or, very traditionally, with lemon juice and caster sugar on Shrove Tuesday.

However you want to serve yours, let your children help to make them and, best of all, toss them.

110 g (4 oz) plain flour
1 egg, beaten
300 ml (½ pint) whole milk
butter for cooking
salt

1 Put the flour into a mixing bowl with a pinch of salt. Make a well and mix in the beaten egg with a balloon whisk until you have a smooth paste. Gradually add the milk while beating continually.

2 Melt a little butter in a small frying pan (it needs to be fairly hot) and add enough batter to cover the bottom of the pan. When the batter begins to bubble, toss your pancake and cook the other side.

This makes about 10 pancakes. They are best served warm, straight out of the pan but you can make them in advance, particularly if you are filling them and re-heating them in the microwave.

Jane Cozens, Mummy to George & Edward

Strawberry and Clotted Cream Sandwiches

 Family food   😊 8 months   🎞 No cooking

This is a fruity teatime treat that children really can make themselves. It was sent to me by the Food & Drink Editor of *Country Living* magazine. Sophisticated simplicity at it's best.

thickly sliced white bread
clotted cream
fresh strawberries, hulled and sliced
sugar

1 Take thick slices of soft white bread with a thin, crisp crust and spread them with lashings of clotted cream.

2 Strew half of the bread slices generously with slices of ripe strawberries, dust with sugar and top with the remaining bread slices.

Shona Crawford Poole, Food & Drink Editor, *Country Living* magazine

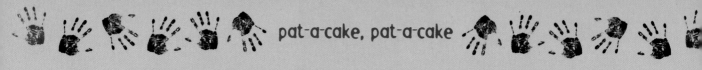

Fruity Chocolate Crispies

 Kid's food 12 months 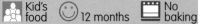 No baking

Children enjoy making this perennial favourite as much as we all enjoy eating them.

110 g (4 oz) milk chocolate, broken into pieces
50 g (2 oz) fruity Special K (with raspberries, cherries & strawberries)
25 g (1 oz) unsalted butter
1 tsp golden syrup
12 paper cake cases

Start by preparing the baking tray. Younger children will love laying out the little paper cases on a baking tray so let them get thoroughly involved in this while you prepare the other ingredients.

This bit needs adult supervision. Gently melt the chocolate in a heatproof bowl set over a pan of barely simmering water (don't let the bowl touch the water) for around 5 minutes or until smooth.

Pick out 12 pieces of dried fruit from the cereal for decoration.

Remove the chocolate from the heat, stir in the butter until it has melted, then add the golden syrup.

Fold in the Special K ensuring that it is well coated and spoon it into the paper cases, decorating with the reserved fruit.

Leave in the fridge to set for about 2 hours.

You can, of course, use other cereals such as Rice Crispies or cornflakes to make these delicious chocolate treats.

Try making Easter Nests by placing 3–4 mini eggs on top of each Fruity Chocolate Crispie cake before chilling.

Lorna Wing, Mummy to Charlie and food writer for *Sainsbury's Magazine*

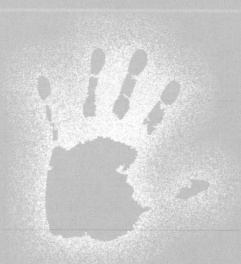

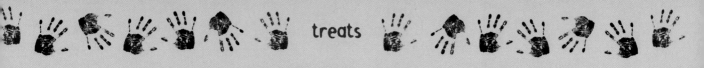
Choccy Didgy Biccy Cake

 Family food   😊 12 months   🎞 No baking

In compiling *Cooking with Daisy*, I was sent many versions of this recipe under various aliases. Some people know it as Tiffin, others simply call it Chocolate Biscuit Cake. As a child, I knew it as Broken Biscuit Cake. But I feel the best name for this yummy biscuit cake is Choccy Didgy Biccy Cake, so that's what we'll call it. It's a great recipe for kids to get involved in, they love breaking up the biscuits that form the foundation for the cake. It can also be made very quickly and requires no cooking, so provides almost instant gratification for impatient chefs.

100 g (3½ oz) unsalted butter
3 tbsp golden syrup
25 g (1 oz) cocoa powder
200 g (7 oz) chocolate digestive biscuits
100 g (3½ oz) milk or plain chocolate for icing

Melt the butter gently over a low heat and stir in the syrup and the cocoa powder.

As the butter melts (don't let it burn), you need to smash the digestive biscuits up into crumbs. Put the biscuits into a strong plastic bag and then hit it repeatedly with a rolling pin.

Once you are happy with the size of your crumbs – don't let over-enthusiastic hammering get the better of the kids – take your pan off the heat and gently fold the biscuit crumbs into the melted chocolate mixture using a wooden spoon. You can also add one or two handfuls of raisins at this stage if you wish but I think that pure, unadulterated Choccy Didgy Biccy Cake is the best. Once the crumbs are well coated, pour them into a well-buttered shallow baking tray and flatten it out with your wooden spoon so that it becomes quite solid. It now needs to go into the fridge to set (about 20–30 minutes).

Melt the chocolate in a heatproof bowl over a pan of barely simmering water (don't let the bowl touch the water) and spread it on top of the now cooled biscuit cake. Chill again until the chocolate sets or for as long as you can resist.

Jules Pick, Mummy to Joey & Tom

Gingerbread Men (or Women!)

Kid's food | 12 months | 8–10 mins baking

For children, the best thing about gingerbread men (apart from the eating) is the decoration at the end. With this recipe, you will need thin paint brushes dipped in golden syrup for the glue. Then you can stick on sweets or cake decorations to make the faces. The whole thing becomes a very sticky, gooey mess but is great fun.

This makes around 6–7 gingerbread men, depending on the size of your cutter.

50 g (2 oz) butter
1 tbs milk
2 tbsp golden syrup
115 g (4 oz) flour
50 g (2 oz) soft brown sugar
1 tsp ground ginger
½ tsp ground cinnamon

To decorate:
golden syrup
selection of sweets & cake decorations

1. Preheat the oven to 180°C (fan 160°C), 350°F or Gas Mark 4 and grease a large baking tray.

2. Place the butter, milk and golden syrup in a small saucepan and heat gently until the butter has melted.

3. Mix together the flour, sugar, ginger and cinnamon in a large bowl and make a well in the centre.

4. Pour the melted butter mixture into the dry ingredients and mix into a ball with a wooden spoon. Now leave the dough in the bowl to cool thoroughly before rolling it out.

5. Once it is cool, flour a rolling pin and roll the dough out onto a floured surface to about 5 mm (¼ inch) thick. Cut out your gingerbread men, using a shaped cutter, or create any other gingerbread shapes that your child may fancy. Transfer the shapes to your greased baking tray with the help of a palate knife. Bake for 8–10 minutes.

6. Leave the gingerbread men to cool a little and then transfer to a wire rack. When thoroughly cooled, decorate to your heart's content.

Elly Bailey, Mummy to Honor

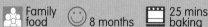

Chocolate Brownies

👪 Family food   🙂 8 months   🗓 25 mins baking

These are seriously good and seriously easy to make. They can be served as they come or with ice cream for a fantastically indulgent pudding.

55 g (2 oz) plain chocolate
115 g (4 oz) butter
2 eggs
225 g (8 oz) caster sugar
70 g (2½ oz) plain flour

1. Preheat the oven to 180°C (fan 160°C), 350°F or Gas Mark 4 and line the bottom of a greased, low-sided baking tray.

2. Start by melting the butter and chocolate together in a mixing bowl set over a pan of barely simmering water (don't let the bowl touch the water).

3. While you are waiting for them to melt (don't forget to stir occasionally), beat the eggs. Once the chocolate and butter have liquefied, mix the eggs, sugar and flour into the liquid.

4. Pour the mixture into the baking tray and bake for roughly 25 minutes. Allow to cool for 5 minutes and then turn out onto a wire rack to cool thoroughly. Once cool, cut into about 16 little squares.

Harriet Thompson, Mummy to Claudia, Elsie & Grace

Traditional Flapjack

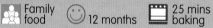

👪 Family food   🙂 12 months   🗓 25 mins baking

I can never resist flapjacks. This is so easy to make that it hardly needs describing but here goes.

300 g (10½ oz) butter
200 g (7 oz) soft brown sugar
1 tbsp golden syrup
400 g (14 oz) rolled oats

1. Set the oven to 180°C (fan 160°C), 350°F or Gas Mark 4 and melt the butter, sugar and syrup in a large saucepan, taking care not to let it boil.

2. Stir in the oats and press the mixture into a well-buttered, low-sided baking tray and bake for 25 minutes.

3. Take the cooked flapjack out of the oven and mark the surface up into squares or fingers using a sharp knife. It is important to do this before it becomes brittle so that it's easy to break into pieces.
To vary this basic flapjack recipe, try adding either a small handful of sultanas or a little crispy cereal.

Gilly Hollway, Granny to Oliver & William

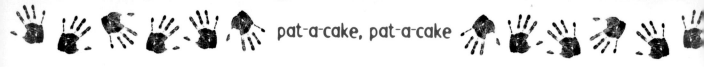

pat-a-cake, pat-a-cake

Chewy Gooey Flapjack

Family food 😊 **12 months** 🎬 **25–30 mins baking**

This is a twist on traditional flapjack that includes bananas so, while it's a treat, they are also getting some of their recommended daily fruit intake.

140 g (5 oz) butter
100 g (3½ oz) light muscovado sugar
2 heaped tbsp golden syrup
350 g (12 oz) porridge oats
1 level tsp ground cinnamon
½ tsp baking powder
2–3 medium bananas, mashed
salt

The preparation is as easy as with traditional flapjack.

1. Preheat your oven to 160°C (fan 140°C), 325°F or Gas Mark 3.

2. Melt the butter, sugar and syrup in a pan, stir in the oats, cinnamon, baking powder and a pinch of salt.

3. Add the mashed bananas and stir in well and then press the mixture into a well-buttered, low-sided baking tray and bake for 25–30 minutes or until they are golden brown. Mark out portions with a knife while the flapjack is still warm and then, when it has cooled slightly, move it onto a wire rack to cool.

Alternatively, these can be made into individual flapjacks; make rounds with your hands and then flatten them slightly onto a buttered, flat baking sheet. This will make around 12 of these individual flapjacks.

Rona Stuart-Bourne, Mummy to Edward, Louis, Annabel & Marcus

Grandma's Drop Scones

Family food · ☺ 12 months · 3–5 mins frying

Don't confuse these with Ruth Watson's traditional Teatime Scones (see page 188) although both should be made at least once and I promise that you'll make them again. These are a totally different kettle of fish – flat pancakes filled with raisins that should be served hot and smothered in butter on a cold and rainy afternoon.

225 g (8 oz) plain flour
1 level tsp bicarbonate of soda
1½ level tsp cream of tartar
3 level dessertspoons caster sugar
1 egg
just less than 300 ml (½ pint) milk
oil for cooking
a handful of raisins

1. Mix all of the dry ingredients, except the raisins, in a bowl and make a well in the centre.

2. Beat the egg and milk together and pour into the well. Beat the batter until it becomes smooth and then add the raisins. You can add as few or as many as you wish or even none at all. It's entirely up to you.

3. Kids love watching the next bit – the transformation from mixture to drop scone – but make sure they stand well back from hot pans. You need to grease a frying pan with a wad of oil-soaked kitchen paper and then drop the mixture in, a tablespoonful at a time. One spoonful will make one drop scone and you should be able to fit 3 or 4 at a time into most pans without them running into each other.

4. Once they've been cooking for a short time, you'll see bubbles appear all over the upper side. At this point, you need to flip them over with a palate knife and cook the underside for roughly the same amount of time. They should be lightly browned on both sides.

Cover them with butter while still hot and eat immediately. You can, of course, store them in an airtight container and heat them for a very short time in a microwave to serve them hot on another occasion.

For a delicious savoury version that can be served for lunch or tea with either sausages or crispy bacon, leave out the sugar and substitute the raisins for a small can of drained sweetcorn.

Kerry de Lanoy Meijer, Mummy to Charlie & Alice

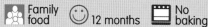

Chocolate Refrigerator Cake

👥 Family food   🙂 12 months   🎛 No baking

This is an extremely sophisticated Choccy Didgy Biccy Cake (see page 179) and, as such, is also incredibly popular with grown-ups. Ideal for Mothering Sunday or Father's Day when children want to make something for their parents.

200 g (7 oz) packet natural glacé cherries, halved
2 tbsp cranberry juice
150 g (5½ oz) bar dark chocolate with fruit (Green & Black's Dark Chocolate
    with Whole Cherries is superb), broken into pieces
200 g (7 oz) Bournville chocolate, broken into pieces
175 g (6 oz) butter, cut into eight pieces, plus extra for greasing
100 g (3½ oz) golden syrup
200 g (7 oz) packet digestive biscuits

1. Grease a 20 cm (8 inches) loose-based round tin and line the base with baking paper. Put the glacé cherries into a bowl, cover them with the cranberry juice, then leave to soak.

2. Put all the chocolate, the butter and golden syrup in a large microwave-proof bowl. Cook on Medium (in a 900w oven) for 2 minutes, then stir and cook for a further 2 minutes until the chocolate has melted. (Alternatively put the chocolate, butter and syrup into a bowl and melt over a pan of barely simmering water, making sure the bottom of the bowl doesn't touch the water.)

3. Put the biscuits into a food processor and whiz to crush roughly or let your children have a really good bash at them using a rolling pin and tough plastic bag.

4. Add half the soaked cherries and all the biscuits to the chocolate mixture, then stir. Spoon into the tin and level the surface.

5. Arrange the remaining cherries around the edge of the cake. Chill until set before serving. To serve, remove from the tin and peel off the baking paper. Cover and store for up to 2 weeks in the fridge.

Lindsay Nicholson, Editor-in-Chief, *Good Housekeeping*

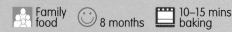

Proper Teatime Scones

Family food · 8 months · 10–15 mins baking

This recipe was sent to me by Ruth Watson who owns the award-winning Crown & Castle Hotel in Suffolk. There is an art to making a great scone as she explains...

'You can make scones with ordinary milk but buttermilk gives them a pleasant, slightly tart flavour, as well as extra lightness. Lard, too, sounds very old-fashioned and politically incorrect, but there's not very much — anyway if you're worried about fat, better to go easy on the whipped cream. The dough should be neither dry, tight and crumbly, nor too loose and sticky: a soft, pliable, tender dough, that has not been pummelled too much, is the foundation of a splendidly crusty-but-tender scone. Unfortunately, it's almost impossible to give the exact amount of liquid required because it all depends on the age, make and temperature of the flour you use, but start off with three-quarters of the carton of buttermilk and dribble in more as needed.'

Scones do not keep very well and are best eaten within a few hours of being made. If you have to make them in advance, freeze them. This makes about 12 large scones.

450 g (1 lb) self-raising flour
1 tbsp caster sugar
55 g (2 oz) lard, softened
55 g (2 oz) unsalted butter, softened
284 ml (10 fl oz) carton buttermilk

1. Preheat the oven to 230°C (fan 210°C), 450°F or Gas Mark 8.

2. Combine the flour and sugar in a large mixing bowl, then rub in the fats — using both hands in a thumb-and-two-finger, quick, pinching action — until the texture is like breadcrumbs. Add the buttermilk cautiously, again using your hands to mix it to a soft dough.

3. Dust a work surface with flour and roll the dough out to a thickness of about 4 cm (1½ inches), handling it as little as possible. Don't worry if it looks a little craggy. Take a 6 cm (2½ inch) biscuit cutter and cut out as many scones as possible, making sure the cuts are quick, hard and direct. Gather the dough scraps into a ball, re-roll and cut out more scones.

4. Put the scones onto a heavy baking sheet (ungreased), and bake them on the middle shelf for 10 minutes. Reduce the heat to 190°C fan 170°C), 375°F, Gas Mark 5, and continue to cook for 10–15 minutes, or until the scones are well-risen and a light golden brown.

Serve them as soon as possible with bowls of clotted or whipped double cream, and richly-flavoured red fruit jam, such as strawberry, raspberry, morello cherry or damson.

I adore scones and occasionally make bite-sized ones using about a 2.5 cm (1 inch) biscuit cutter. These deliciously tiny treats are great served piled with jam and cream at parties — but remember to halve the baking times recommended for Ruth's larger Teatime Scones.

Ruth Watson, award-winning cookery writer and owner of the Crown & Castle Hotel in Suffolk

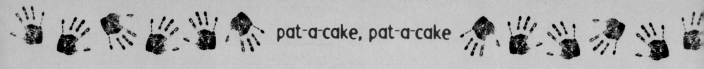

Peppermint Creams

 Family food   12 months   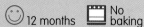 No baking

These are really easy and fun for children to help make – think of the mixture as edible play dough! They make perfect presents too and look great wrapped in coloured cellophane.

1 egg white
350 g (12 oz) sifted icing sugar
peppermint essence
green food colouring (optional)

Whisk the egg white until it is frothy.

Beat in about two-thirds of the icing sugar and then add a drop or two of the peppermint essence and also a drop of the food colouring (if you're using it).

Turn the mixture out on to a clean working surface and knead in the remaining icing sugar. Check the flavour. Add more peppermint if necessary.

Roll out the mixture to about 5 mm (¼ inch) thick and then use small round or shaped cutters to create the peppermint creams.

Leave on greaseproof paper to set firm.

Sarah Littlefair, Mummy to Charlie

Chocolate Truffles

 Family food   12 months   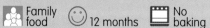 No baking

Children will scarcely need adult help with these incredibly simple truffles.

100 g (3½ oz) sweetened chocolate powder + extra for rolling
60 g (2¼ oz) butter, softened
icing sugar

Blend the chocolate powder into the softened butter with a wooden spoon.

Using your hands, mould the mixture into little marble-size balls and roll them in either icing sugar or more chocolate powder to cover them. If the mixture gets too hot and sticky in little hands, simply chill it for a moment or two and start again.

Place them carefully in a box to create a perfect homemade gift. Keep refrigerated.

Millionaire's Shortbread

Family food | 12 months | 30–40 mins baking

This does represent quite a culinary commitment, since it has to be made in three stages. All are very simple but you do need to plan ahead. That said, it absolutely has to be made and makes an irresistible gift for sweet-toothed grannies or perfect party food.

For the shortbread layer:

175 g (6 oz) butter
225 g (8 oz) plain flour
75 g (3 oz) caster sugar

Preheat the oven to 170°C (fan 150°C), 325°F or Gas Mark 4.

Rub the butter into the flour and sugar. This can be done by hand and children will really enjoy feeling the different textures as they are combined. However, if time is tight pop it all into the food processor until you have a loose ball.

Put the mixture into a well-buttered baking tray with sides and press it into the tray so that it is well lined using your hands. Finally, prick it with a fork.

Bake it in the preheated oven for 5 minutes and then turn the oven down to 150°C (fan 130°C) 300°F or Gas Mark 2 for a further 30–40 minutes or until golden brown.

Leave it to cool before adding the caramel.

For the caramel layer:

200 g (7 oz) butter
379 g can condensed milk
4 tbsp golden syrup

This absolutely has to be done under a watchful eye since it gets very, very hot. Melt the butter in a pan and stir in the condensed milk and golden syrup. You then need to let this mixture bubble on full heat until it changes colour, gets thick and boils. You must keep stirring to prevent it from burning.

Pour the mixture onto the shortbread and leave to cool and set before adding the chocolate.

For the chocolate layer:

300 g (10½ oz) dark or milk chocolate (whichever you prefer)

You can do this very easily in the microwave. Break up your chocolate, put it in a microwaveable container and cook for about 1 minute until it has all melted. If you don't have a microwave, put pieces of chocolate in a heatproof bowl over a pan of barely simmering water (don't let the bowl touch the water), stirring until it has melted.

Pour the chocolate evenly over the caramel layer and leave to set.

Just before the chocolate sets, cut the shortbread into squares. You'll find it much easier to cut this way. It's extremely rich so I would recommend about 2.5 cm (1 inch) squares.

Camilla Geffen, Mummy to William, Edward & Harry

Quercus Publishing Ltd
21 Bloomsbury Square, London, WC1A 2NS

First published 2006
This paperback edition 2007

Text copyright © Josie Klafkowska 2006
Photographs copyright © Pip Calvert 2006
Design copyright © Quercus Publishing Ltd 2006
Copy-edited and proofread by: Lin Thomas
Design: Neal Cobourne
Editorial and project management:
JMS Books LLP

All rights reserved. No part of this publication
may be reproduced, stored in a retrieval system,
or transmitted in any form or by any means,
electronic, mechanical, photocopying, recording
or otherwise, without the prior permission in
writing of the copyright owners.

The views expressed in this book are those
of the author but they are general views only
and readers are urged to consult a relevant
and qualified specialist for individual advice
in particular situations. Josie Klafkowska and
Quercus Publishing Ltd hereby exclude all liability
to the extent permitted by law for any errors or
omissions in this book and for any loss, damage or
expense (whether direct or indirect) suffered by a
third party relying on any information contained
in this book.

A catalogue record for this book is available from
the British Library.

ISBN 1 84724 160 3
ISBN-13 978 1 84724 160 3

Printed and bound in China.